PRESSURE COOKER RECIPES

Quick & Easy Pressure Cooker Recipes for Easy Meals

(The Essential Quick and Simple Pressure Cooker Cookbook)

James Prather

Published by Sharon Lohan

© **James Prather**

All Rights Reserved

Pressure Cooker Recipes: Quick & Easy Pressure Cooker Recipes for Easy Meals (The Essential Quick and Simple Pressure Cooker Cookbook)

ISBN 978-1-990334-25-2

All rights reserved. No part of this guide may be reproduced in any form without permission in writing from the publisher except in the case of brief quotations embodied in critical articles or reviews.

Legal & Disclaimer

The information contained in this book is not designed to replace or take the place of any form of medicine or professional medical advice. The information in this book has been provided for educational and entertainment purposes only.

The information contained in this book has been compiled from sources deemed reliable, and it is accurate to the best of the Author's knowledge; however, the Author cannot guarantee its accuracy and validity and cannot be held liable for any errors or omissions. Changes are periodically made to this book. You must consult your doctor or get professional medical advice before using any of the suggested remedies, techniques, or information in this book.

Table of contents

Part 1	1
Introduction	2
Pressure cooker potato salad	3
Italian chicken soup	5
Pot roast	7
Carnitas	9
Sausage, kale, and white bean soup	11
Kidney bean curry	13
Cabbage tamales	16
Red lentil and yellow split pea soup	18
Mensaf (Jordanian lamb stew)	20
Hummus	22
Hard boiled eggs	24
Mashed potatoes	26
Kosher chicken soup with matzo balls	28
Shredded pork taco filling	31
Cream of carrot soup	33
Rasgullas	35
Khara Pongal	37
Cream of tomato soup	39
Italian rice croquettes	41
Spicy red beans with fennel seed	43
Conclusion for Pressure Cooker Recipes	45
Chicken Cacciatore	47

- Stuffed peppers 49
- Cheesy chicken and rice 51
- Beef stew 53
- Dinners 55
- One Dish Chicken Onion Stew 55
- Cooker Carnitas 56
- Saucy Pressurized Beef Stew 58
- Pressure Cooker Teriyaki Wings 60
- Pressure Pork with Plum Sauce 62
- Tender Beets with Walnuts 64
- Pressure Cooker Jambalaya 66
- Potato Pressure Soup 68
- Pressure Kakuni 70
- Pressure Cooker Tomato Calamari 72
- Chicken Pressure Cooker Soup 74
- Cabbage and Corned Beef One Pot Dinner 75
- Chicken Risotto 77
- Lamb Shanks Cooked in Tomato Celery Sauce 79
- Brussels Sprouts with Bacon 81
- Sausage Red Bean Stew 82
- Shrimp Risotto 84
- Easy Pulled Pork 86
- Pressure Cooker Steak 88
- Chicken Lentil Soup 90
- Pressure Cooker Herb Roast Chicken 91
- Cooker Pepper Ribs 92
- Lemon Zest Artichokes 94

Moist Shredded Chicken	96
Pressure Cooker BBQ Ribs	98
Chicken Alfredo	100
Bean Ham Pressure Soup	102
Honey Chicken	104
Chicken with Dumplings	106
Noodles with Meatballs	108
Simple Cooker Lasagne	109
Mashed Potatoes	111
Beef Stroganoff	112
Pressure Cooked Beef Pho	114
Pork Pressure Ragu	117
Asparagus Thyme Risotto	118
Pork Chops in Mushroom Sauce	120
Meatballs in Tomato Gravy	121
Black bean Garlic Soup	123
Beef Ribs Cooked in Cola Sauce	125
Desserts	127
Peach Cobbler	127
40 Minute Dulce De Leche	131
Walnut Banana Cake	132
Decadent Chocolate Cheesecake	134
Lava Cake	136
Rice Pudding	138
Chocolate Mousse	140
Carrot Halva	142
Blueberry Delight	144

Part 2 146
Have You Heard Of The Instant Pot? 147
How To Choose The Right Instant Pot 150
Is An Instant Pot Worth The Money? 153
Instant Pot vs. Slowcooker 155
Breakfast, Lunch, And Dinner In The Instant Pot 157
Unusual Ways To Use Your Instant Pot 159
The Instant Pot Saves Time And Money 162
Is The Instant Pot Safe? 164
How To Find Instant Pot Recipes 167
Stuffed Peppers 170
Spaghetti And Meatballs 172
Quick Shredded Buffalo Chicken Sandwiches 174
One Pot Creamy Chicken & Rice 175
Quick Leftover Chicken Pizza 176
Easy Peasy Roast 177
Southwest Chicken Soup 178
Garlic Herbed Chicken 179
Leftover Vegetable Soup 181
Philly Cheese Steak Sandwiches 182
Chicken Alfredo with Pasta 183
Swiss Steak 185
Jambalaya 186

Part 1

Introduction

Welcome to this beginners recipe guide to pressure cooking, where you will discover how to whip up the most amazing pressure cooker recipes which will save you time and money, and make family friendly home meals.

If you have never experienced using pressure cooker meals, then you will be blown away with what you will discover inside this quick and easy recipe book.

Inside I will teach you the little known tips and tricks to get the best results from your pressure cooker recipes which will save you hours of time trying to figure it out on your own.

Enjoy!

Pressure cooker potato salad

By making this salad you'll reduce the time it takes to make traditional potato salad and your potatoes will still be nice and firm!

Ingredients

- Six medium red potatoes, scrubbed
- One cup water
- One fourth cup chopped onion
- One stalk celery, chopped
- Salt
- Pepper
- Three hard-boiled eggs, chopped
- One tablespoon chopped fresh dill
- One half cup mayonnaise
- One teaspoon yellow mustard
- One teaspoon cider vinegar

Instructions

1. Place the potatoes in the pressure cooker with water. Cook on high pressure for three minutes. If the potatoes are large cook for four minutes.

2. Let the pressure cooker release steam for three minutes. Quickly release the pressure and open the cooker. Peel and dice the potatoes once you can safely handle them.
3. Alternate the layers of potatoes, onion, and celery in a large bowl. Season each layer with salt and pepper.
4. Top with chopped egg and sprinkle with dill.
5. In a separate bowl mix the mayonnaise, mustard, and cider vinegar. Gently pour the mayonnaise mixture into the potatoes and stir carefully.
6. Chill for at least one hour before serving.

Italian chicken soup

This is a hearty meal that many people have soon claimed it as a favorite.

Ingredients

- Two teaspoons olive oil
- Four Italian turkey sausage links, casings removed
- One medium onion, diced
- Three cloves garlic, minced
- One half cup pearl barley
- One cup green lentils
- One bone-in chicken breast half, skin removed
- One half cup chopped fresh parsley
- Three cups chicken stock
- One (15 ounce) can chickpeas (garbanzo beans), drained
- One (16 ounce) bag fresh spinach leaves, chopped
- One cup mild salsa

Instructions

1. Heat one teaspoon olive oil in a pressure cooker over medium heat. Add the sausage meat and cook

until browned. Break it up into crumbles. Remove the sausage onto a plate and drain the oil.

2. Add another one teaspoon of olive oil to the pressure cooker. Cook the onion and garlic until the onion is transparent.

3. Add the barley and stir for one minute.

4. Return the sausage to the pressure cooker and add the lentils, chicken, parsley, and chicken stock. Add just enough to cover the chicken.

5. Close the cover securely and place the regulator on the vent pipe. Bring the pressure cooker to full pressure over high heat.

6. Reduce the heat to medium high and cook for nine minutes.

7. Remove the pressure cooker from the heat and use the quick release function following the manufacturer's directions.

8. Open the cooker and remove the chicken. Shred the chicken and return it to the soup. Add the garbanzo beans, spinach, and salsa. Stir to blend and heat before serving.

Pot roast

If you like pot roast this is a simple way to make one and the meat always comes out tender!

Ingredients

- Two tablespoons vegetable oil
- One (three pound) beef chuck roast
- One large onion, diced
- One (one ounce) package dry Italian salad dressing mix
- One (one ounce) package dry Ranch-style dressing mix
- One (1.2 ounce) package brown gravy mix
- One (fourteen and a half ounce) can beef broth

Instructions

1. Keeping the lid open heat the oil inside the pressure cooker over a medium-high heat.
2. Place the roast inside and brown it on all sides in the hot oil.
3. In a small bowl mix together the Italian salad dressing mix, Ranch dressing mix, and gravy mix. Once mixed sprinkle them evenly over the roast.

4. Poor in the beef broth and add the chopped onion.
5. Seal and lock the pressure cooker and cook over a high heat to build pressure until the indicator sounds.
6. Turn the heat down to medium and cook for forty five minutes.
7. Once the forty five minutes have passed remove the pressure cooker from the heat and let stand for five minutes.
8. You can use the juices for gravy by thickening it with flour or cornstarch.

Carnitas

A pressure cooker really packs in the flavor for these carnita tacos. There are many different things you can serve these carnitas with.

Ingredients

- Three tablespoons canola oil
- Three pounds boneless pork shoulder, cut into one and a half inch cubes
- Two fresh poblano peppers, roughly chopped
- Three jalapeno peppers, roughly chopped
- One serrano pepper, roughly chopped
- One large onion, roughly chopped
- Four cloves garlic, roughly chopped
- Two teaspoons ground coriander
- Three teaspoons ground cumin
- One and a half cups beef broth

Instructions

1. Place the oil into the pressure cooker and cook over a medium-high heat. Brown the pork cubes on all sides inside the hot oil.
2. Stir in the poblano, jalapeno, and serrano peppers, onion, garlic, coriander, cumin, and beef broth.

3. Lock the lid on the pressure cooker. Bring the cooker up to pressure and then slowly reduce the heat to keep the pressure steady.

4. Cook under medium steady pressure for one hour. Remove the cooker from the heat and release the pressure. When it is safe remove the lid and serve.

Sausage, kale, and white bean soup

People have often described this soup as a "comforting" one due to the ingredients involved.

Ingredients

- One cup dry navy beans
- One large bunch kale, rinsed, stemmed and chopped
- One tablespoon olive oil
- One pound spicy linguica sausage, sliced
- One cup chopped shallots
- Four cups chicken broth
- Salt
- Pepper
- One half teaspoon hot sauce

Instructions

1. Place the navy beans in a large container and fully cover with cool water. Let stand eight hours or overnight. Drain and rinse the beans before using.
2. Cook the soaked beans in a pressure cooker in four cups of water for twenty five minutes. Use the natural release method to release the pressure. Do not drain!

3. In a separate pot add salt and water and bring to a boil. Add the kale and simmer until the kale is bright green and tender. This should take about two minutes. Drain the kale in a strainer and cool under cold running water. Set aside for now.
4. Heat olive oil over medium heat in a soup pot. Brown the linguica slices on each side for about five minutes. Remove from the pot with a spoon and set aside.
5. Add the shallots to the pot and cook until soft. This should take about three minutes.
6. Pour in a small amount of chicken broth and scrape up any leftover brown bits of sausage.
7. Return the sausage to the pot along with the beans and the liquid used for cooking. Stir in the chicken broth.
8. Bring the soup to a boil, reduce the heat to low, and let simmer uncovered for fifteen minutes.
9. Add the kale and cook for about four more minutes.
10. Season to taste using the salt, pepper, and hot sauce.

Kidney bean curry

This is an inexpensive, nutritious, and comforting type of meal. What more could you ask for?

Ingredients

- Two cups dry red kidney beans
- One large onion, chopped
- Four cloves garlic, chopped
- One (two inch) piece fresh ginger root, chopped
- Two tablespoons vegetable oil
- Two teaspoons ghee (clarified butter)
- Two dried red chile peppers, broken into pieces
- One teaspoon cumin seeds
- One teaspoon ground turmeric
- One teaspoon ground cumin
- One teaspoon ground coriander
- Two tomatoes, chopped
- Two cups water
- One teaspoon white sugar
- Salt
- Two teaspoons garam masala
- One teaspoon ground red pepper

- One fourth cup cilantro leaves, chopped
- Six whole cloves

Instructions

1. Place the kidney beans in a large bowl and cover with cool water. Let stand eight hours or overnight. Drain and rinse.
2. Grind the onion, ginger, and garlic into a paste using a mortar and pestle.
3. Heat the oil and ghee together in a pressure cooker over medium heat. Fry the red chile peppers, cumin seeds, and whole cloves in the hot oil until the cumin seeds begin to splutter. Stir in the onion paste into the mixture and cook, stirring frequently, until a golden brown.
4. Season with the ground turmeric, ground cumin, and ground coriander. Continue cooking for a few more seconds before adding the tomatoes. Cook the tomatoes until they are completely tender.
5. Add the drained kidney beans to the pressure cooker and add enough water to cover. Pour in two additional cups of water.
6. Add the sugar and salt.
7. Close the pressure cooker and bring to fifteen pounds of pressure. Cook for about forty minutes.
8. Lower the heat to low and cook for an additional ten to fifteen minutes.

9. Release the pressure and open the cooker when it is safe.
10. Stir the garam masala and ground red pepper into the bean mixture.
11. Garnish with chopped cilantro and serve.

Cabbage tamales

This is a hearty meal that you can eat at any time!

Ingredients

- Eight cabbage leaves
- One pound ground beef
- One and a half cups uncooked white rice
- Two (six and a half ounce) cans tomato sauce
- Three teaspoons New Mexico red chile powder
- Two cloves garlic, minced
- One half cup chopped onions
- Salt
- Pepper
- Two (ten ounce) cans diced tomatoes with green chile peppers

Instructions

1. Freeze the cabbage leaves or blanch them for about three minutes in a large pot of boiling water to soften.
2. Inside a large bowl add the ground beef, rice, tomato sauce, chile powder, garlic, onion, salt, and

black pepper in a bowl. Mix with your hands until all the items are well combined.

3. Divide the meat mixture into eight portions and place them on the softened cabbage leaves. Toll the leaves to form logs and tuck the edges under the "logs."
4. Place the tamales into a pressure cooker.
5. Pour diced tomatoes with green chiles over the tamales.
6. Seal the lid of the pressure cooker and bring it up to full pressure. Reduce the heat to low and cook for one hour.

Red lentil and yellow split pea soup

This is an easy to make and filling soup. It also comes together very quickly for a quick and easy dinner

Ingredients

- One cup red lentils
- One cup yellow split peas
- One large onion, coarsely chopped
- Two carrots, coarsely chopped
- Five cloves garlic, chopped
- One and a half teaspoons ground cumin
- Eight cups chicken broth
- Salt
- Pepper
- One teaspoon lemon juice, or to taste

Instructions

1. Place the lentils, split peas, onion, carrots, garlic, and cumin into a pressure cooker. Stir in the chicken broth.
2. Seal the cooker and bring to pressure over a medium heat. Reduce the heat to keep the pressure stable and cook under pressure for thirty minutes.

3. Remove from heat and when it is safe remove the cover.
4. Season the soup with salt, pepper, and lemon juice before serving.

Mensaf (Jordanian lamb stew)

This comes close to the national stew of Jordan. It is often eaten on special occasions.

Ingredients

- Four tablespoons olive oil
- Two pounds boneless lamb shoulder, cut into two inch pieces
- Eight cups water
- Two cups uncooked white rice
- One fourth cup pine nuts
- Six pita bread rounds
- One cup salted goat's milk (jameed el-kasih)

Instructions

1. Add one tablespoon olive oil into a pressure cooker over medium-high heat. Add the lamb and cook evenly until browned on all sides. Remove the lamb and add a cooking rack. Place the lamb on the rack and pour in four cups of water.
2. Close the lid tightly and place the pressure regulator on the vent pipe. Bring cooker to full pressure over high heat. Reduce heat to medium-high and cook for forty minutes.

3. Remove the pressure cooker from the heat and allow the pressure to drop. Once safe remove the lamb and separate the meat from the bones. Discard the bones.
4. Pour the pan broth into a bowl and set aside.
5. In a sauce pan add four cups water, one tablespoon olive oil, and the rice into a saucepan. Bring this to a boil over medium-high heat. Stir and reduce the heat. Cover and let simmer until all the moisture is absorbed. This should take about twenty minutes.
6. Place the last two tablespoons of olive oil in a skillet over medium heat. Stir in the pine nuts and cook until a deep brown. This should take about five minutes.
7. Pour two cups of the reserved broth into a large pan. Add the goat's milk and the lamb to the milk-broth mixture. Simmer over medium heat allowing the lamb to absorb some of the liquid. This should take about thirty minutes.

To serve:

Arrange the pita bread on the bottom of a large platter. Spoon the rice over the bread. Place the lamb on top of the rice and drizzle with any remaining milk-broth mixture. Sprinkle pine nuts over the top.

Hummus

If you like hummus now you can make your own!

Ingredients

- Three fourth cup dry garbanzo beans
- One fourth cup dried soybeans
- One bay leaf
- One onion, quartered
- One cup vegetable broth
- Three cups water
- Two cloves cloves garlic, crushed
- One lemon, juiced
- Two tablespoons soy sauce
- Pepper
- One fourth cup tahini
- One fourth cup chopped fresh parsley

Instructions

1. Rinse the garbanzos and soybeans well and place them in a pressure cooker with a bay leaf and onion.
2. Add the vegetable broth and enough water to cover the beans by one inch.

3. Seal the lid securely and bring the pressure up to high. Reduce the heat to low and cook while maintaining high pressure for one hour. After one hour allow the pressure to drop naturally.
4. Drain the beans and save the liquid.
5. Place the beans inside the bowl of a food processor. Add the garlic, lemon juice, soy sauce, black pepper, and tahini; process until smooth. You can add some of the cooking liquid in there for a thinner consistency.
6. Spoon the mixture into a bowl and mix in the parsley.

Hard boiled eggs

If you have chickens or a stream of access to fresh eggs hard boiling them in a pressure cooker is a great way to go!

Ingredients

- Two cups water
- Eight fresh eggs
- Four cups cold water
- Four cups ice cubes

Instructions

1. Fill the pressure cooker with the minimum amount of water that is specified by the manufacturer.
2. Place your eggs in the steamer basket above the water.
3. Seal the lid and bring the pressure cooker up to a low pressure.
4. Cook for six minutes. Remove the pressure cooker from the heat and allow the pressure to drop for five minutes.
5. In a separate bowl combine the cold water and ice in a large bowl.

6. Using the quick-release method to open the pressure cooker move the hot eggs to the ice water using a spoon.
7. Let cool completely for about thirty minutes.

Mashed potatoes

Using this recipe and heating the milk and butter before mashing them in and using a hand masher will yield you fluffy and delicious mashed potatoes.

Ingredients

- Three cups cold water
- Three and a half pounds russet potatoes, peeled and sliced three fourth inch thick
- One fourth cup butter
- One half cup whole milk
- Two teaspoons kosher salt
- One half teaspoon white pepper

Instructions

1. Using high heat inside the pressure cooker bring the water to a boil. When the water is boiling add the potatoes.
2. Seal lid and bring cooker up to high pressure. Reduce heat to low, maintaining high pressure, and cook for thirty minutes.
3. Using the quick-release method to lower the pressure.
4. Drain potatoes and return them to pressure cooker.

5. Next add the butter and milk and cover pressure cooker with lid for five minutes. This allows the heat from the potatoes to melt the butter and warm the milk.
6. Once safe remove the lid and season with kosher salt and white pepper. Use a hand masher to mash the potatoes until the lumps are mostly gone.
7. Transfer to a bowl and serve hot.

Kosher chicken soup with matzo balls

Here is a chicken soup that is full of delicious flavors.

Ingredients

For the Chicken Soup

- One (two and a half to three pound) whole chicken, cut up
- Two small yellow onions, diced
- Two stalks celery, cut into chunks
- Three carrots, cut into chunks
- One bunch fresh dill
- One bay leaf
- Three quarts water

For the Matzo Balls

- One third cup vegetable oil
- Four eggs
- Two tablespoons chopped fresh basil
- One tablespoon chopped fresh parsley
- One and a half teaspoons salt
- One fourth teaspoon ground black pepper

- One cup matzo meal
- Three quarts water
- One teaspoon salt

Instructions

1. Inside the pressure cooker combine the chicken, onions, celery, carrots, dill, bay leaf, and water.
2. Seal the pressure cooker and bring it up to full pressure. Reduce the heat while maintaining full pressure and cook for thirty minutes. Allow the pressure to drop naturally.
3. Remove the chicken and vegetables from broth. Strain the broth and discard the vegetables.
4. When the chicken is cool enough to handle remove the chicken meat from the bones and discard the bones.
5. In a bowl combine the vegetable oil, eggs, basil, parsley, one and a half teaspoons salt, and black pepper and mix well.
6. Stir in the matzo meal and cover the bowl with plastic wrap. Refrigerate for one hour.
7. In a large pot add three quarts of water and one teaspoon of salt and bring to a boil.
8. Using wet hands gently shape the matzo mixture into balls about two inches across and drop them in

the boiling water. Let them simmer for twenty minutes.

9. Skim the fat off the chilled chicken broth and place broth in a pot over medium heat.
10. Add salt to taste and the leftover cooked chicken.
11. Transfer the cooked matzo balls to the chicken soup and heat to serve.

Shredded pork taco filling

Here's a unique way to make your own taco fillings!

Ingredients

- One half teaspoon garlic powder
- Two teaspoons ground cumin
- Two teaspoons ground coriander
- Two teaspoons dried oregano
- One fourth teaspoon cayenne pepper
- One (three and a half) pound pork shoulder roast
- Four cups beef broth
- Two bay leaves
- One half large white onion, cut into large chunks

Instructions

1. In a bowl mix the garlic powder, cumin, coriander, oregano, and cayenne pepper.
2. Take this mix and thoroughly rub it over the pork.
3. Place the pork in a pressure cooker with the beef broth, bay leaves, and onion over medium-high heat.
4. Seal the cooker and bring to full pressure. Reduce the heat to maintain high pressure and cook for forty five minutes.

5. Remove the pressure cooker from the heat and allow the pressure to drop naturally.
6. Place the pork to a serving bowl and shred the meat with forks.
7. Serve in a tortilla or a taco.

Cream of carrot soup

This is a creamy soup that is sure to please!

Ingredients

- One fourth cup butter
- Two and a half cups diced onions
- One large Yukon Gold potato, peeled and diced
- One and a half cups roughly chopped celery
- Six green onions, chopped
- Eight cloves garlic
- Six cups baby carrots
- Ten cups vegetable stock
- Four cups heavy whipping cream
- One half teaspoon mild curry powder
- Salt
- Black pepper

Instructions

1. Set the pressure cooker to a medium heat and melt the butter.
2. Add and stir the onions and salt in the hot butter until the onions become translucent. This should take about ten minutes.

3. Add the potato, celery, green onions, and garlic and cook until slightly tender. This should take three to five minutes.

4. Add the carrots and vegetable stock and increase heat to high.

5. Place the lid on and set for fifteen pounds of pressure. Once it is to pressure reduce the heat to medium-high and cook for seven minutes.

6. Remove the cooker from the heat and release the pressure. Once it is safe remove the lid.

7. Stir the cream and curry powder into soup.

8. Transfer the soup to a blender and puree it until it is smooth.

9. Season to taste with salt and black pepper.

Rasgullas

If you ever were intimidated by the idea of making rasgullas before you don't need to be anymore! Here is an easy and great recipe so you can now make them whenever you wish.

Ingredients

- Six cups milk
- Three tablespoons fresh lime juice
- Two and a half cups white sugar
- Six cups water
- One teaspoon ground cardamom

Instructions

1. Using a heavy-bottomed pan bring the milk to a boil till it starts foaming. Immediately add the lime juice and stir. It will curdle right away and that is normal. You should see the milk solids (chenna) separate from the whey. Pour this mixture into a colander lined with cheesecloth and rinse the chenna with cold water to get rid of the lime juice. Be sure to allow the water to drain completely.

2. Gather the muslin cloth edges like a parcel and expel as much water as possible. What you now have is soft paneer. Turn the paneer onto a rolling mat or other smooth surface and knead the paneer

well to make a smooth paste. Roll this into a ball and divide into twenty equal portions.

3. In your pressure cooker bring the water to a boil. Stir the sugar into the boiling water until it has dissolved.

4. Carefully roll each portion of paneer into a smooth ball between your palms and make sure there are no cracks. Once that is done gently drop the balls into the hot syrup.

5. Secure the lid onto the pressure cooker and bring to pressure. Reduce heat to medium-low and pressure cook for six minutes.

6. Release the pressure from the cooker and remove the lid when it is safe.

7. The rasgullas should be floating on top of the syrup and have expanded to two or three times in size.

8. Pour the rasgullas and syrup into a bowl. Gently stir the cardamom into the mixture.

9. Place in your refrigerator to chill completely before serving cold.

Khara Pongal

Pongal is a classic pooja dish in south India. If you wish to try something new this is a great place to start.

Ingredients

- One fourth cup cooking oil
- Twelve cashews
- Two dried red chile peppers
- One teaspoon cumin seed
- One teaspoon mustard seed
- Ten black peppercorns
- One pinch asafoetida powder
- One cup split yellow lentils (moong dal)
- One cup rice
- One half cup shredded coconut
- Two green chile peppers, chopped
- One half teaspoon ground turmeric
- Salt
- Three and a half cups water
- Two tablespoons ghee
- One fourth cup chopped cilantro leaves
- One fourth cup shredded coconut

Instructions

1. Heat the oil in the pressure cooker. Add the cashews and fry them in the hot oil until golden brown. Remove them from oil and set aside.
2. Add the red chile peppers, cumin seed, mustard seed, peppercorns, and asafoetida and cook them in the hot oil for two minutes.
3. Stir the lentils into the mixture and cook another two minutes.
4. Next add the rice, one half cup coconut, green chile peppers, turmeric, salt, and water and stir.
5. Close the lid of the cooker and bring to fifteen pounds of pressure and cook for thirty five minutes.
6. Relieve the pressure from the cooker and when it is safe stir the stir the cashews and ghee into the mixture.
7. Garnish with the cilantro and one fourth cup shredded coconut to serve.

Cream of tomato soup

With this soup you can have all the delights of having cooked all day with none of the hassle!

Ingredients

- Four cups peeled, seeded, and cored tomatoes with juice
- One cup chicken broth
- One and a half teaspoons salt
- One half teaspoon baking soda
- One and a half cups milk
- One half cup heavy whipping cream
- Salt
- Black pepper

Instructions

1. Inside the pressure cooker combine the tomatoes with juice, chicken broth, and salt.
2. Cover and bring to medium pressure for three minutes. Carefully use quick-release to release pressure and remove lid.
3. When it is safe stir baking soda into tomato mixture until it is no longer bubbling.

4. Next add the milk, cream, salt, and pepper to tomato mixture.

5. Using a hand held blender blend the soup well.

6. Heat soup over medium-low heat and stirring often for about fifteen minutes.

7. Remove from the heat source and ladle into bowls.

Italian rice croquettes

If you enjoy Italian food here's a great recipe to use for parties or whenever you feel like it!

Ingredients

- Two pounds chicken giblets
- One cup water
- One half teaspoon salt
- Four cups salted water
- Two cups long grain white rice, uncooked
- Two cups grated Parmesan cheese
- One half cup marinara sauce
- One fourth cup dry bread crumbs
- Two large eggs
- Two tablespoons chopped fresh parsley
- Salt
- Black pepper
- One cup dry bread crumbs for coating
- Vegetable oil for frying

Instructions

1. Inside the pressure cooker combine the chicken giblets, one cup water, and one half teaspoon salt in a pressure cooker. Cook for about twenty minutes.
2. After twenty minutes have passed drain giblets and let them cool for about ten minutes. Chop giblets up in a food processor or by hand and set aside.
3. In a large sauce pan bring the rice and water to a boil over high heat. Reduce heat to medium-low, cover the sauce pan, and let simmer until the rice is tender and the liquid has been absorbed. This should take twenty to twenty five minutes.
4. Spread the cooked rice onto a baking sheet to cool for about five minutes. After five minutes have passed transfer the rice to a large bowl.
5. In the bowl with the rice mix in giblets, grated Parmesan cheese, marinara sauce, one fourth cup bread crumbs, eggs, parsley, salt, and ground pepper. Cover the bowl with plastic wrap and refrigerate for one hour.
6. After one hour has passed remove the rice and giblet mixture from refrigerator and form two inch football shaped croquettes. Roll the croquettes in bread crumbs and place on a baking sheet.
7. Heat the oil in a large skillet over medium-high heat and cook the breaded croquettes until browned on all sides. This should take about ten minutes.
8. Transfer the croquettes to a plate lined with paper towels to absorb excess oil and serve warm.

Spicy red beans with fennel seed

This meal goes great with cubed ham or red beans and rice.

Ingredients

- Two cups dry kidney beans
- Two teaspoons salt
- One and one half teaspoons fennel seed
- One half teaspoon cayenne pepper
- Freshly ground mixed peppercorns to taste

Instructions

1. Place the beans inside the pressure cooker and fill with enough water to cover the beans by one inch. Bring this to a boil and boil it for two minutes.
2. After two minutes have passed remove the cooker from the heat, drain, and let cool for one hour.
3. After one hour has passed add water once again to the beans but this time have just enough water to cover the beans by one half inch.
4. Season with this mixture with salt, fennel seed, cayenne pepper and mixed peppercorns.
5. Place the lid on the cooker and set the pressure to fifteen pounds. Bring to a boil and cook for thirty five minutes.

6. Release the pressure and wait until it is safe to remove the lid.
7. Serve hot.

Conclusion for Pressure Cooker Recipes

Thank you again for downloading this book! I hope you've enjoyed reading about all the great pressure cooker recipes available for you to try.

Make sure you also check out my other recipe books which are always full of fresh new ideas to help you benefits from this tasty way of life.

The next step is to take action on what you have learned today. I'm sure with the right practice and listening to my directions step by step of the way you will become a pressure cooking pro in no time!

Finally, if you enjoyed this book, then I'd like to ask you for a favor, would you be kind enough to leave a review for this book on Amazon? It'd be greatly appreciated!

How Crockpot cooking work and how to get set up

A crock pot is also often known as a "slow cooker". There are several different types of crock pots including the basic models with "low" and "high" settings that are accompanied by a "keep warm" setting after the amount of specified time has passed. There are several advanced models where a person can specifically program in an allotted amount of time and temperature but these can be much more expensive.

Setting up your crock pot does not have to be a difficult process. To be able to set it up properly you will need to be aware of the different parts of your crock pot.

1. **The lid**. This is one of the first parts of your crock pot that should always stay on your crock pot unless the recipe specifies otherwise.
2. **Ceramic bowl**. This is the bowl that goes into your crock pot base. It is often ceramic or some form of material that can withstand the heat. This part you can safely wash.
3. **Base**. This is metal and often has all your knobs and things on it. You **cannot** wash this!

If you don't like washing dishes there are crock pot liners that you can find at your local grocery store. These line the ceramic bowl and where you put all your items inside. They are not necessary but they can be beneficial as you will be less likely to have to clean up any sticky mess afterwards.

You only want to fill your crock pot **three-fourths** of the way full. **Do not** fill it all the way to the top as this can lead to spillage and it can damage your crock pot.

Crock pots are handy things to have and it is very easy to make tasty meals with them. Best of all you don't have to be standing over a stove all day to make them!

Twenty great tasting crock pot recipes!

Here I shall be giving you twenty different recipes for tasty meals that just seem to cook themselves!

Chicken Cacciatore

If you like chicken and have some left over noodles this is a great recipe to try.

Ingredients

- One and a half pounds skinless chicken breasts
- Three to four garlic cloves, minced
- Twenty eight ounces diced tomatoes
- Six ounces tomato paste
- One half red bell pepper, sliced
- One half green bell pepper, sliced
- One small onion, diced
- One teaspoon dried oregano
- One teaspoon dried basil
- One teaspoon salt
- One half teaspoon pepper
- One bay leaf
- One fourth cup water
- One package pasta

Instructions

1. Season the chicken breasts with the salt and pepper or via your preferred method. Add the other ingredients **except** for the pasta and stir well to combine.
2. Cover and set the crock pot on low for seven hours or on high for four hours.
3. Prepare your pasta via your preferred method.
4. Once the chicken is done cooking serve it on top of the cooked pasta.

Stuffed peppers

If you enjoy stuffed peppers or wish to try something new here is a great place to start!

Ingredients

- Six large bell peppers
- One and a half pounds raw ground chuck beef
- Two cups chicken or vegetable stock
- One (15 ounce) can of diced tomatoes
- One medium onion chopped
- Twi cloves garlic, minced
- Twi cups shredded cheddar cheese
- One egg
- One teaspoon salt
- One half teaspoon pepper

Instructions

- Cut the tops off the peppers and remove the seeds and ribs from the inside.
- In a large mixing bowl combine the ground beef, cooked rice, one half of the can of chopped tomatoes, onion, garlic, cheese, egg, salt and pepper. Mix this blend well.

- Carefully scoop out and place this mixture well into the peppers. Place these peppers inside your crock pot. Add in the rest of the tomatoes around them.
- Cover and cook on high for five to six hours or on low for eight hours.

Cheesy chicken and rice

This is a simple recipe that many will enjoy.

Ingredients

- One (eight ounce) box Zatarain's Yellow Rice, cooked according to the package
- Four boneless skinless chicken breasts
- Two cups shredded cheddar cheese
- One medium onion, chopped
- One (ten and a half ounce can) can cream of chicken soup
- One (fifteen ounce) can of corn, drained
- Two cups chicken stock

Instructions

1. Spice the chicken breasts with salt and pepper before placing into the crock pot. Sprinkle the chopped onions on top of the chicken.
2. Mix well the two cups of chicken broth and can of cream of chicken soup and pour the mixture over the chicken.
3. Cover and cook on low for seven to eight hours or on high for four hours.
4. Before serving shred the chicken with two forks.

5. Add the cooked and prepared rice, cheese, and corn. Mix until well blended and the cheese has melted.

Beef stew

Stew is an excellent dinner for those cold winter months or if you need something filling.

Ingredients

- Two pounds beef stew meat, cut into cubes
- One teaspoon salt
- One teaspoon pepper
- One medium onion, finely chopped
- Two celery ribs, sliced
- Two to three cloves of garlic, minced
- Six ounce can tomato paste
- Thirty two ounce beef broth
- Two tablespoons Worcestershire sauce
- Two cups baby carrots
- Four to five small red potatoes, cut into cubes
- One tablespoon dried parsley
- One teaspoon oregano
- One cups frozen peas
- One cup frozen corn
- One fourth cup flour
- One fourth cup water

Instructions

1. In a large crock pot combine the beef, celery, red onion, carrots, potatoes, salt, pepper, garlic, oregano, parsley, Worcestershire sauce, beef broth, and tomato paste. Cover and cook on low for ten hours or on high for six to seven hours.
2. About half an hour before it is done cooking mix the flour and water in a small dish and pour into the crock pot. Mix well until it combines. Next add the frozen peas and corn. Cover once again and cook for thirty minutes.

Dinners

One Dish Chicken Onion Stew

Prep Time: 5 minutes

Cooking Time: 30 minutes

Servings: 4 persons

Ingredients

- 1 large onion, sliced into ¼ inch slices
- 4 large Russet or Yukon Gold potatoes, peeled and cut into 1-2 inch chunks
- 1 whole chicken, back removed, cut into 8 pieces (about 4 pounds), or 4 whole chicken legs, cut into thighs and drumsticks
- 4 medium beefsteak tomatoes, cut into 1- to 2-inch chunks (about 3 cups)
- Kosher salt and freshly ground black pepper
- 2 bay leaves

Directions

1. Place all ingredients in the pressure cooker, seal firmly and cook for 25 minutes on medium heat.
2. Wait for steam to escape, open lid, taste the seasonings and serve hot.

Cooker Carnitas

Prep Time: 10 minutes

Cooking Time: 1 hour 30 minutes

Servings: 12 persons

Ingredients

- 3 pounds boneless pork shoulder, cut into 1 1/2-inch cubes
- 3 tablespoons canola oil
- 2 fresh Poblano peppers, roughly chopped, or more to taste
- 1 serrano pepper, roughly chopped, or more to taste
- 3 jalapeno peppers, roughly chopped, or more to taste
- 1 large onion, roughly chopped
- 2 teaspoons ground coriander
- 1 ½ cups beef broth
- 4 cloves garlic, roughly chopped
- 3 teaspoons ground cumin

Directions

1. Heat oil in a pressure cooker over medium heat. Brown the pork cubes and then add jalapeno, Poblano, Serrano pepper, garlic, onion, coriander, beef broth and cumin and mix well.

2. Close the cooker lid firmly, reduce heat and ensure the pressure is steady.
3. Cook for one hour, and then take off heat. Let the steam escape slowly, open the lid carefully and serve.

Saucy Pressurized Beef Stew

Prep Time: 10 minutes

Cooking Time: 35 minutes

Servings: 15 persons

Ingredients

- 3 teaspoons cooking oil
- 9 pounds rump steak or 9 pounds chuck roast
- 3 onions, chopped
- 3 carrots, chopped
- 2 cups diced celery
- 3 bay leaves
- 2 cups sliced mushrooms
- 1 teaspoon salt
- 2 10½-ounce cans beef broth
- 3 (6 ounces) cans tomato paste
- 1 ½ cups dry red wine

Directions

1. Heat the pressure cooker, add meat and brown on all sides.
2. Toss in the seasonings and vegetables. And mix with meat.
3. In a bowl mix the paste with wine and broth and pour into pressure cooker.
4. Close the cooker with lid securely.

5. Cook at medium heat for 35 minutes. Switch off gas, let it steam escape slowly.
6. Remove the lid and if you do need thicker gravy, boil without lid for a few more minutes and serve hot.

Pressure Cooker Teriyaki Wings

Prep Time: 10 minutes

Cooking Time: 20 minutes

Servings: 4 persons

Ingredients

- 6 tablespoons sesame oil OR (vegetable oil)
- 2-3 pounds chicken wings, drum and wings separated
- 1 tablespoon lemon juice
- ½ teaspoon crushed red pepper, toasted sesame seeds for garnish
- 1 cup low sodium teriyaki sauce
- 2 Tablespoons Sugar

Directions

1. Take a Zip Lock bag; add in chicken wings, teriyaki sauce, sesame oil, sugar and lemon juice and leave to rest in refrigerator for 2 hours.
2. Heat a pressure cooker, pour 2 tablespoons of sesame oil, add chicken wings without the marinade and brown on all sides.
3. Finally pour the marinade and place the lid securely and cook on high heat for 10 minutes. Once the whistle comes, switch off the gas and let the pressure escape before opening the lid.

4. Carefully take out wings, arrange the wings on a baking sheet lined with foil and bake for 10 minutes at 400F.
5. Serve with crushed red pepper and toasted sesame seeds.

Pressure Pork with Plum Sauce

Prep Time: 10 minutes

Cooking Time: 70 minutes

Servings: 4 persons

Ingredients

- 2 tablespoons soy sauce
- 3 to 4-pound pork shoulder roast, cut into 1 1/2" to 2" cubes, trimmed of as much fat as possible
- 1 teaspoon vegetable oil
- 4 cloves of garlic, peeled and smashed
- 1 onion, chopped
- 1-inch fresh ginger, grated
- 2 cups chicken stock
- 2 scallions, trimmed and cut into 1 inch lengths
- 2 tablespoons soy sauce
- 2 cups pitted dried plums
- 1 tablespoon seasoned rice vinegar or dry sherry

Directions

1. Season pork and heat a large pan. Sear pork on both sides for one minute each and place in a plate. Do this in batches.
2. Heat 1 teaspoon oil in the pressure cooker, and once again sear pork for 2 minutes on each side and work in batches.

3. Place browned pork in a plate and drain off oil from the cooker but leave 2 tablespoons inside the cooker.
4. Sauté ginger, garlic, scallions until they are soft. Pour chicken stock and let it boil.
5. Scrape the bottom to mix in any fried bits of pork into the gravy.
6. Now add plums, seared pork, soy sauce, vinegar and mix well.
7. Close the pressure cooker firmly, reduce the heat and cook for 15 minutes.
8. Take off from heat, release the steam quickly, open lid, skim off fat from the surface and drain pork onto a serving plate.
9. Reduce the gravy until it thickens to a sauce consistency.
10. Check seasoning, pour more vinegar and soy sauce if you need and finally slowly pour the sauce over pork and serve warm.

Tender Beets with Walnuts

Prep Time: 10 minutes

Cooking Time: 10 minutes

Servings: 4 persons

Ingredients
- 2 pounds beets (about 6)
- 1 tablespoon cider vinegar
- 2 ½ cups water
- 1 tablespoon fresh lemon juice
- 1 ½ teaspoons Dijon mustard
- 2 teaspoons sugar
- ¾ teaspoon kosher salt
- 3 tablespoons extra-virgin olive oil
- 2 tablespoons finely chopped walnuts
- ½ teaspoon freshly ground black pepper
- 2 tablespoons chopped fresh dill

Directions
1. Brush and clean the beetroot. Leave about 1 inch of its stem and the root on.
2. Pour 2 ½ cups of water in a pressure cooker, place in the beetroots, and close the lid properly.
3. Boil on high heat and cook for 10 minutes. After that, leave to rest and allow the steam to escape.

4. Rinse the beets in cold water, slice off the roots, and cut the beets vertically into half and then each half into 4 wedges.
5. Place the wedges in a bowl, and mix in the other ingredients, except walnuts and toss well.
6. Finally add walnuts and serve fresh.

Pressure Cooker Jambalaya

Prep Time: 10 minutes

Cooking Time: 30 minutes

Servings: 4-6 persons

Ingredients

- ½ pound boneless skinless chicken breasts, cut into 1" pieces
- 1 tablespoon vegetable oil
- ½ pound fully cooked Andouille or Italian sausage, sliced
- 2 teaspoons Creole seasoning
- ½ pound uncooked shrimp, peeled and deveined
- 1 teaspoon dried thyme leaves
- 3 garlic cloves, minced
- 1/8 teaspoon cayenne pepper
- 1 green bell pepper, chopped
- 1 cup long grain rice
- 1 onion, chopped
- 3 stalks celery, sliced
- 16 ounces canned chopped tomatoes, not drained
- 3 tablespoons fresh parsley, minced
- 1 cup chicken stock

Directions

1. Heat oil in a pressure cooker on medium heat. Toss in shrimp, chicken and sausage. Add half the Creole seasoning and stir well.
2. Once they are cooked, remove into a bowl and set aside.
3. Now into the cooker, add celery, onion, Creole seasoning, and bell pepper and cook for 5 minutes.
4. Then add tomatoes, their juices, rice, reduce heat and cover and cook
5. The time should be long enough to ensure the rice is cooked as per the instructions.
6. Once cooked, let the steam get released and then open the lid.
7. Mix in chicken, parsley, shrimps and sausages and cover it once again tightly for 5 minutes before serving.

Potato Pressure Soup

Prep Time: 15 minutes

Cooking Time: 20 minutes

Servings: 4-6 persons

Ingredients

- 1 can chicken broth
- 1 can cheddar cheese soup
- 1 pound grated cheddar cheese
- 1 soup can milk
- 4 cups whole milk
- 2 tablespoons butter
- ½ teaspoon salt
- 2 tablespoons cornstarch
- ½ teaspoon pepper
- ½ teaspoon garlic salt
- ½ teaspoon onion powder
- 7 medium potatoes, diced to 1 inch

Directions

1. Place potatoes in pressure cooker, add 2 cups water and secure the lid on firmly. Let it cook for about 4 whistles, wait for the steam to escape and then open it.
2. Now open lid of cooker, add soup, 1 can milk, ½ the broth, and combine. Pour the rest of the milk and all

the cheese. Mix cornstarch in a little broth to a smooth paste and pour into soup.
3. Next add butter and spices and boil for 20 minutes.
4. Stir well and serve warm with a garnish of bacon bits and chives.

Pressure Kakuni

Prep Time: 5 minutes

Cooking Time: 45 minutes

Servings: 4 persons

Ingredients
- 1-inch ginger
- 3 green onions (we'll use only the green parts)
- 2 pounds pork belly block
- 1 tablespoon vegetable oil
- Water for cooking pork belly
- Shichimi Togarashi (Japanese 7 spices) for taste
- 4 boiled eggs

Seasonings
- ½ cup water
- ¼ cup sake
- ½ cup mirin
- ¼ cup sugar
- ½ cup soy sauce

Directions
1. Slice the green parts into half, peel the ginger and slice into thin slices. Keep the white onion parts away for later use.
2. Open the stove top pressure cooker, pour oil and heat it. Add the pork belly and stir until oil coast all the sides.

3. Pour water into cooker, add ginger and green onions. Seal the lid firmly and let it cook at high heat for first 5 minutes, then reduce to medium heat and cook for 30 minutes. Let steam escape through the vent about 4-5 times.
4. Once cooked, switch off the heat, let the pressure escape slowly.
5. Take out the pork belly, rinse in warm water and keep aside. Drain the cooking liquid from the pressure cooker into a bowl.
6. Now place the pork belly back into the pressure cooker, add the seasonings and mix gently. Add boiled eggs and let it get sautéed over medium heat without lid on.
7. Once the alcohol in the pressure cooker evaporates, put on the lid, bring down to simmering heat and let it cook for 10 minutes. Let the steam escape through the vent about 3-4 times.
8. Now open after all the pressure escapes and ensure that the liquid has thickened and condensed to nearly half the original quantity.
9. Serve pork belly with rice and pour the sauce over the rice and enjoy with any vegetables, boiled eggs and a dash of theShichimi Togarashi if you like.

Pressure Cooker Tomato Calamari

Prep Time: 15 minutes

Cooking Time: 30 minutes

Servings: 4 persons

Ingredients

- 1 ½ pounds calamari fresh or frozen, thawed and drained
- ½ cup of white wine
- 14.5 ounces can of chopped tomatoes
- 1 clove garlic, smashed
- chopped 2 anchovies
- 1 bunch parsley,
- 1 lemon, juiced
- 1 pinch red pepper flakes
- olive oil salt & pepper

Directions

1. To clean the calamari- first detach head from the top hat of calamari. Carefully pull out the inner parts joined to the head.
2. Rinse in water and gently tear out skin from the hat and clean the the hat and flesh inside out.
3. While washing you will feel a stiff quill. Once you catch the end that is sticking out from the hat, tug it and pull it out.

4. Keep the hat in a bowl and then move on to the tentacles. W only need the tentacles and throws the rest away.
5. Feel the inner cartilage like bone that runs through the tentacles, just squeeze and pull out the flesh.
6. Now wash the tentacles, the hat and head once again and slice into thin strips. Keep aside.
7. To cook the calamari- Heat the pressure cooker, pour 2 tablespoons of oil, garlic, anchovies and hot pepper. Reduce heat to the lowest setting, add calamari and mix everything well.
8. Pour wine and boil for 3 minutes. Next add, chopped tomatoes, measure water in the tomato can and pour into cooker, add parsley and stir everything well.
9. Secure the pressure cooker lid firmly, raise the heat to highest, and cook for 20 minutes.
10. Take off heat, let the pressure get released, open lid and squeeze lime juice, and a drizzle of olive oil and some more parsley into the calamari mix, stir and serve hot.

Chicken Pressure Cooker Soup

Prep Time: 10 minutes

Cooking Time: 10 minutes

Servings: 4-5 persons

Ingredients
- 3 pieces chicken breast, cubed (a little over a pound)
- 3 ribs of celery, sliced
- ½ onion, diced
- 3 large carrots, sliced
- 1 ½ teaspoons dried thyme
- 1 tablespoon butter
- ½ teaspoon salt or season to taste
- 2 ½ cups uncooked extra wide noodles
- ¼ teaspoon pepper or season to taste
- 7 cups chicken broth or 7 cups of water mixed with 7 teaspoons of Chicken Base

Directions
1. Rub pepper into the cubed chicken. Melt some butter in the pressure cooker.
2. Brown the chicken in the cooker, and take off heat.
3. Add thyme, onions, carrots, celery, salt, uncooked noodles, pepper and broth mix into the pressure cooker and mix well with the browned chicken.

4. Place it back on heat, close the lid firmly. Cook on high heat for 10 minutes. Release pressure gently and then serve in bowls.

Cabbage and Corned Beef One Pot Dinner

Prep Time: 5 minutes

Cooking Time: 2 hours

Servings: 6 persons

Ingredients
- 1 corned beef brisket (3-4 pounds)
- 1 small onion, peeled and quartered
- 4 cups water
- 3 garlic cloves, peeled and smashed
- 3 whole black peppercorns
- 2 bay leaves
- ½ teaspoon whole allspice berries
- 1½ pounds small or medium red potatoes
- 1 head cabbage, cut into wedges
- 1 teaspoon dried thyme
- 5 medium carrots, peeled and cut into chunks

Directions
1. Heat the pressure cooker; add everything except carrots, potatoes and cabbage.
2. Close with lid carefully, and cook on medium heat for the first 10 minutes and then reduce and cook for 80 minutes.

3. Take off heat; take time to release the pressure from the cooker and transfer meat into a large bowl or plate.
4. Now add in cabbage, potatoes and carrots into the cooking hot liquid in the pressure cooker and cook for 10 minutes at medium heat with lid on.
5. Once done, release the steam and place the vegetables and pour the liquid over meat and serve hot.

Chicken Risotto

Prep Time: 10 minutes

Cooking Time: 10 minutes

Servings: 4 persons

Ingredients
- 2 pounds chicken thigh fillets, trimmed, cut into 1" pieces
- 2 tablespoons olive oil
- 1 brown onion, finely chopped
- 1 ½ cups Arborio rice
- 2 garlic cloves, finely chopped
- ½ cup dry white wine
- ¾ cup grated parmesan, plus extra to serve
- 3 ¼ cups chicken stock
- 3 ounces baby spinach
- 1-ounce butter, diced

Directions
1. Heat half the oil in a pressure cooker and cook chicken in 1-3 batches. It should get browned on all sides. Place the browned chicken on a plate.
2. Pour the rest of the oil in the cooker, add onion and stir until soft. Then add garlic, and stir until fragrant. Next toss in rice and stir until opaque.
3. Place the chicken back, pour wine and stock and combine everything.

4. Latch the lid on firmly and cook on high heat for 5 minutes. Then reduce to low and cook for another 5 minutes.
5. Take off heat, let the steam release on its own. Remove the lid, add butter, parmesan and place the lid back on. Leave undisturbed for 5 minutes so that the rice absorbs the butter, cheese and any liquid.
6. Finally add spinach, season if needed, stir and top with cheese when serving.

Lamb Shanks Cooked in Tomato Celery Sauce

Prep Time: 10 minutes

Cooking Time: 45 minutes

Servings: 4 persons

Ingredients

- 3 pounds lamb shanks
- Freshly ground black pepper
- Kosher salt
- 2 tablespoon ghee, divided
- 2 celery stalks, roughly chopped
- 2 medium carrots, roughly chopped
- 1 large onion, roughly chopped
- 3 cloves garlic, smashed and peeled
- 1 tablespoon tomato paste
- 1 pound ripe roma tomatoes or 14 ounce can of diced tomatoes
- 1 teaspoon Red Boat Fish Sauce
- 1 cup bone broth
- ¼ cup minced Italian parsley (optional)
- 1 tablespoon aged balsamic vinegar

Directions

1. Rub salt and pepper onto the shanks and keep aside.
2. Heat the pressure cooker with ghee and add the lamb shanks. Brown it evenly on all sides.

3. Chop vegetables. Once lamb is browned, remove onto a platter and toss in the vegetables into the pressure cooker.
4. Once the vegetables are a bit soft, add tomato paste, garlic cloves and stir well. Place shanks back into cooker, add tomatoes, bone broth, fish sauce, pepper and balsamic vinegar and stir well.
5. Firmly seal with the lid and heat over high heat for 5 minutes. Then bring down to simmering heat and cook for 40 minutes.
6. Once cooked, wait for the pressure to escape and serve in a plate with a fresh garnish of parsley.

Brussels Sprouts with Bacon

Prep Time: 5 minutes

Cooking Time: 10 minutes

Servings: 4-6 persons

Ingredients

- ½ cup bacon, diced very small
- 1 tablespoon Dijon mustard
- 1 pound Brussels sprouts, trimmed and cut in half
- 1 cup chicken or vegetable broth
- 1 tablespoon butter
- 2 tablespoons fresh chopped dill

Directions

1. Heat the pressure cooker on medium to high heat, add bacon and cook for 2 minutes.
2. Add Brussels sprouts, mustard, chicken broth, mix and place lid on securely. Cook for 5 minutes on high heat.
3. Once pressure has been released after cooking, add butter, dill, salt and pepper and mix well before serving.

Sausage Red Bean Stew

Prep Time: 10 minutes

Cooking Time: 40 minutes

Servings: 4 persons

Ingredients
- 1 pound of dried red beans, washed
- 2 tablespoons Cajun seasoning homemade
- 2 pounds spicy sausage, cut into bite sized pieces
- 2 celery stalks, chopped
- ½ onion chopped
- 1 green pepper
- salt and pepper
- 1 teaspoon dried parsley
- About 5 cups of water, enough to cover ingredients.
- ½ teaspoon ground cumin

Cajun seasoning
- 2 teaspoons salt
- 2 teaspoons paprika
- 2 teaspoons pepper
- 3 teaspoons garlic powder
- 1 ½ teaspoons of cayenne pepper
- 2 teaspoons onion powder
- 1 ½ dried thyme
- 1 ½ dried oregano
- red pepper flakes for additional heat

Directions

1. Mix all the Cajun seasonings together and store in an airtight container. It will last for about 3 months.
2. Chop the sausages and vegetables, and place into the pressure cooker. Stir a bit until vegetables are soft.
3. Throw in the spices, pour enough water to cover everything well. Combine well.
4. Seal with lid, and cook on medium heat for 30 minutes. Let the pressure release slowly, open lid and serve.

Shrimp Risotto

Prep Time: 10 minutes

Cooking Time: 15 minutes

Servings: 4 persons

Ingredients
- 4 tablespoons unsalted butter, divided
- 2 garlic cloves, minced
- 1 small yellow onion, finely chopped
- 1 ½ cups Arborio rice
- 4 ½ cups low-sodium chicken broth, divided
- 2 tablespoons dry white wine, such as Sauvignon Blanc or Pinot Grigio
- 1-pound large shrimp, peeled and deveined (21 to 30)
- Coarse salt and freshly ground pepper
- ¼ cup fresh herbs such as tarragon and flat-leaf parsley, chopped
- ¾ cup grated Parmigiano-Reggiano cheese (3 ounces), plus more for serving

Directions
1. Heat the pressure cooker, melt 2 tablespoons of butter, add garlic and onions and sauté until soft and fragrant. Throw in rice, and stir for 1 minute. Pour wine, cook until alcohol evaporates.
2. Next pour 3 cups broth, pepper and salt, place lid on and place on medium to high heat.

3. Cook for 10 minutes. Take off from heat, remove lid after pressure has been released, ad shrimps, 1 ½ cups broth and cook until shrimps are just cooked.
4. Stir in more butter and cheese and garnish with herbs and serve hot.

Easy Pulled Pork

Prep Time: 10 minutes

Cooking Time: 75 minutes

Servings: 8 persons

Ingredients
- 7 pounds pork shoulder
- 2 tablespoons olive oil
- 1 bottle beer
- 2 medium onions
- 7-10 cloves garlic
- ½ cup white vinegar
- ½ cup white wine
- 4 tablespoons brown sugar
- 4 bay leaves
- 4 tablespoons Worcestershire sauce
- Some liquid smoke
- 1 ½ cups water

Rub:
- 1 teaspoon Hot Paprika
- 2 Tablespoons Brown Sugar
- 1 teaspoon Chili Powder
- Dash Cayenne
- 1 teaspoon garlic powder
- Salt and Pepper to taste

BBQ Sauce

- 1 cup rice vinegar
- 2 teaspoons Frank's hot sauce
- 2 Tablespoons brown sugar
- Salt and Pepper
- 2 teaspoons red pepper flakes

Directions

1. Take the pork butt, trim off any excess fat that you don't like, but not too much as the more fat softens the meat and highlights the spice flavors a lot.
2. Apply the rub onto the pork butt. Heat the pressure cooker with a little olive oil.
3. Once hot, add the pork butt and brown in 1-2 batches. Remove once it has slightly browned. Next add chopped onions, garlic, and sauté until soft.
4. Pour beer, white vinegar, white wine, sugar, Worcestershire sauce, liquid smoke and bay leaves and let it boil.
5. Once the alcohol has evaporated, add the browned meat back, pour water and swirl the cooker gently.
6. Seal the lid on firmly and cook at medium heat for 50-60 minutes.
7. Meanwhile prepare the BBQ sauce- Mix the BBQ sauce ingredients in a bowl and keep aside. It will be a bit runny, but prefect for the pulled pork.
8. Once the pork is done, let the steam release on its own. Open the lid, then shred the pork with a fork and pour the BBQ sauce. Mix well
9. Enjoy pulled pork with some salad and bread.

Pressure Cooker Steak

Prep Time: 10 minutes

Cooking Time: 20 minutes

Servings: 4 persons

Ingredients

Rub:
- 2 teaspoons onion powder
- Salt
- Pepper
- 2 teaspoons cayenne pepper

Others
- 2 tablespoons cooking oil
- 3 cups broth or water
- All spices and herbs you like to add to the broth

Directions
1. Rub the spice mix on to the rib eye steak pieces.
2. Heat oil in the pressure cooker. Sear the steak for 2 minutes on each side. Once seared, take steak out

and keep aside on a plate. Cover the plate with foil paper.
3. Pour broth and any spices you like in to the pressure cooker and boil it. Place the steak back in the cooker and seal the lid firmly.
4. Reduce heat and cook for 10-15 minutes. Remove steak after the pressure has escaped and place on a serving platter.
5. Now serve up the steak with your preferred set of steamed vegetables and rice or bread.

Chicken Lentil Soup

Prep Time: 10 minutes

Cooking Time: 25 minutes

Servings: 4 persons

Ingredients

- 1 pound dried lentils
- 7 cups water
- 12 ounces boneless skinless chicken thighs, all fat trimmed
- 2 tablespoons chicken Better than Bouillon
- 2 scallions, chopped
- 1 small onion, chopped
- ¼ cup chopped cilantro
- 1 medium ripe tomato, diced
- 3 cloves garlic
- 1 teaspoon garlic powder
- ¼ teaspoon oregano
- 1 teaspoon cumin
- ½ teaspoon kosher salt, plus more to taste
- ½ teaspoon paprika

Directions

1. Mix in all the ingredients in a pressure cooker and cook on medium heat for 15 minutes.
2. Let the pressure escape on its own, open lid, shred meat and serve in bowls.

Pressure Cooker Herb Roast Chicken

Prep Time: 10 minutes

Cooking Time: 35 minutes

Servings: 10 persons

Ingredients

- 1 whole - 4 pounds organic chicken
- 1 teaspoon paprika
- 1 tablespoon coconut oil
- 1 ½ cups chicken broth
- ¼ teaspoon freshly ground black pepper
- 1 teaspoon dried thyme
- 2 tablespoons lemon juice
- 6 cloves garlic, peeled
- ½ teaspoon sea salt

Directions

1. Clean and rub the chicken with paprika, salt, pepper, thyme inside and outside the chicken properly.
2. Heat oil in the pressure cooker, add chicken and cook for 7 minutes on all sides.
3. Pour broth, garlic cloves, lemon juice into the cooker.

4. Seal with lid, and cook for 25 minutes on high.
5. Once the time is over, let the steam escape on its own.
6. Then only open and place carefully in a large plate before carving.

Cooker Pepper Ribs

Prep Time: 15 minutes

Cooking Time: 60 minutes

Servings: 2 persons

Ingredients
- ½ rack (about 1 ½ pounds) spareribs
- Freshly ground black pepper
- 1 teaspoon kosher salt
- 1 cup beef stock
- 3 tablespoons packed brown sugar
- 3 tablespoons Dijon mustard

Directions
1. Cut the ribs in a way they can fit into the pressure cooker.
2. Rub into the ribs and keep aside.
3. Heat the pressure cooker, pour beef stock. Then place a steamer inside the cooker.

4. Place the ribs in the steamer. Put on lid, bring to high heat and cook for 20 minutes and then 10 minutes on medium heat.
5. Open lid after the pressure has been released naturally. Take out the ribs, place on a sheet pan lined with foil paper.
6. Boil the liquid in the pressure cooker to thicken a bit.
7. Meanwhile preheat the broiler, place the sheet pan on a rack. Cook for 10 minutes until it browns.
8. Into the thickening sauce in the cooker, stir in brown sugar and mustard and boil until it resembles thick syrup.
9. Baste the ribs with thick sauce and broil for 2 minutes on each side.
10. Serve hot.

Lemon Zest Artichokes

Prep Time: 10 minutes

Cooking Time: 10 minutes

Servings: 4 persons

Ingredients

- 2 cups water
- 2 medium-sized artichokes
- 2 teaspoons minced fresh shallots
- 2 teaspoons fresh lemon zest
-

Dipping sauce

- ½ cup mayo
- 2 tablespoons fresh lemon juice
- ½ cup sour cream or light sour cream

Directions

1. Place metal rack at the bottom of the pressure cooker. Pour 2 cups water and let it boil.
2. Cut any discolored artichoke stems and other leaves and then peel off the thick skin. Slice lengthwise into 2 halves.
3. Then gently remove the inner choke and other remains inside and clean with water.
4. Drop shallots and lemon zest in the boiling water. Place the slices artichokes face down. Lock the lid firmly.

5. Cook for 6 minutes. Take off heat, quickly release the steam carefully.
6. Open lid and pierce with a fork to check if done. If not cooked, place back in cooker and cook for 4 more minutes.
7. Beat the dipping sauce ingredients well and serve with artichokes.

Moist Shredded Chicken

Prep Time: 10 minutes

Cooking Time: 45 minutes

Servings: 4 persons

Ingredients
- 1-pound chicken breast (skinless, boneless pieces)
- ½ onion, finely diced
- 2 cloves of garlic, minced
- ⅓ cup soy sauce
- 1 tablespoon oil
- ⅓ cup white vinegar
- 1 tablespoon black peppercorns
- 3 tablespoon jam
- ¾ cups water

Sauce Thickening Ingredients
- 3 teaspoon water
- 2 teaspoon cornstarch

Directions
1. Heat the pressure cooker, and add all the ingredients till sauce thickening ingredients into the cooker, seal the lid and cook on medium heat for 35 minutes
2. Let the steam escape on its own, then shred the meat with a fork. Transfer contents to a bowl and keep warm.

3. Simmer the liquid in the pressure cooker for 5 minutes on high heat.
4. Mix the sauce thickening ingredients and pour into the liquid. Stir continuously to attain a smooth thick sauce.
5. Pour over shredded chicken, mix and serve with rice.

Pressure Cooker BBQ Ribs

Prep Time: 10 minutes

Cooking Time: 50 minutes

Servings: 4 persons

Ingredients

- 3 ½ pounds St. Louis Ribs
- ½ cup whiskey
- 2 ½ cups barbeque sauce
- ½ cup water
- ¼ cup molasses, not blackstrap
- 2 teaspoons liquid smoke
- 1 teaspoon smoked paprika
- 1 teaspoon onion powder
- 1/4 teaspoon cayenne
- 1/2 teaspoon black pepper
- 1 teaspoon salt

Directions

1. Rinse and dry the ribs with a cloth.
2. Gently slice the skirt meat from the bone as it helps to remove the extra fat and meat.
3. Next, break the membrane from the bone.
4. With the help of towels, grab the ribs, and pull off the membranes on top. Do not pull off the membrane nearer to the ribs as they help the ribs to stay intact,

5. Now cut in between each rib and leave only very little meat around it. Keep flipping and turning and tearing off the membranes as much as possible.
6. Rinse them and place the ribs in the pressure cooker.
7. Into a bowl, add whiskey, barbecue sauce, smoke, water, paprika, cayenne, onion powder, pepper and salt. Pour on the ribs and mix well.
8. Seal the lid firmly and cook on high heat for 30 minutes.
9. Preheat the broiler.
10. Once the ribs are done, take them out and place on a sheet lined with foil. Take out with the help of tongs.
11. Broil for 5 minutes per side.
12. Meanwhile boil the liquid in the pressure cooker for about 10 minutes.
13. Pour this sauce over ribs and broil for 2 minutes per side.
14. Serve warm and store any extra sauce in the refrigerator.

Chicken Alfredo

Prep Time: 10 minutes

Cooking Time: 15 minutes

Servings: 2-3 persons

Ingredients

- 1 15-ounce jar of Alfredo sauce
- 8 ounces dried pasta, egg noodles or fettuccine
- 2 teaspoons chicken base
- 1 cup (fresh or frozen) precooked chicken (dice into ¼" squares, then measure)
- 1 tablespoon roasted garlic
- Parmesan cheese for garnish (optional)
- ½ teaspoon coarsely ground pepper

Directions

1. If you are using precooked chicken, dice about 1 cup of chicken pieces and store the rest in the refrigerator.
2. Pour 2 cups of cold water, and chicken base and pasta (broken into halves or thirds) into the pressure cooker. Boil until pasta is just cooked.
3. If you are using fresh uncooked chicken add along with uncooked pasta, close the lid firmly and cook on high for 5 minutes.
4. Take off heat and let the steam escape.

5. Drain out cooking liquid into a bowl and place the pasta and chicken (if you had added it) to another bowl.
6. Mix in roasted garlic and Alfredo sauce and cooked chicken pieces (if not added earlier), pepper and shredded parmesan cheese and serve hot.

Bean Ham Pressure Soup

Prep Time: 10 minutes

Cooking Time: 40 minutes

Servings: 4-6 persons

Ingredients

- 1-pound dry navy beans
- 2 tablespoons oil
- 8 cups chicken broth
- ⅓ cup carrots, diced
- 1 onion, diced
- 3 celery stalks, diced
- Black pepper to taste
- 1 tablespoon minced garlic
- 1 cup ham, diced

Directions

1. Heat the pressure cooker, clean dry beans (that has been soaked for one hour), and water to cover the beans. Close the lid firmly and cook on medium heat for 12 minutes. Let it release steam on its own. Open and pour contents into a bowl.
2. Pour oil in the cooker; add onions and sauté until soft and light brown. Then toss in celery, carrots, garlic and sauté for 5 minutes. Last add ham, and sauté, then add drained beans, 8 cups liquid and black pepper and stir well.

3. Put on lid and cook on medium heat for 20 minutes. Open once done, and with a ladle measure out 1 cup of bean and liquid only- no ham.
4. Puree this beans and liquid with an immersion blender and pour back to soup. Stir and it will thicken.
5. Serve into bowls.

Honey Chicken

Prep Time: 10 minutes

Cooking Time: 10 minutes

Servings: 4 persons

Ingredients

- ¼ cup Dijon mustard
- 2 pounds boneless, skinless chicken breasts or thighs
- ¼ cup coarse whole grain mustard
- 2 tablespoons light brown sugar
- 3 tablespoons honey
- ½ teaspoon salt
- 1 cup chicken stock or broth
- ¼ teaspoon onion powder

Directions

1. Into the pressure cooker, place chicken.
2. Mix the rest of the ingredients except broth in a bowl and pour over chicken. You will get a nice glaze.
3. Pour half of the glaze and the broth over chicken. Lock the lid on firmly and cook on high heat for 10 minutes.

4. Let the pressure cooker rest and release the pressure on its own.
5. Take out chicken with tongs form the cooker and arrange on a plate. Spread the rest of the glaze over chicken and serve warm.

Chicken with Dumplings

Prep Time: 10 minutes

Cooking Time: 30 minutes

Servings: 4 persons

Ingredients

- 4 boneless, skinless chicken breasts
- 1 can cream of chicken soup
- 2 tablespoons butter
- 1 can chicken broth
- Seasoning to taste
- 1 can refrigerated biscuits
- Chives or parsley for garnish

Directions

1. Place chicken in pressure cooker and spread the butter chunks on top of them. Pour broth and soup. Lock lid and cook for 10- 15 minutes on medium heat.
2. Remove the pressure quickly, take out the chicken chunks and cut them into small pieces. Place pieces back into cooker.
3. Take the biscuits and cut each into 9 parts and add to chicken.
4. Put the lid back on and cook for 5 minutes on high heat.

5. Release pressure quickly, and add seasonings, chives or some parsley and stir lightly. The biscuit should not be raw in the center and if it is, then put the lid back on for 5 minutes more.
6. Serve hot.

Noodles with Meatballs

Prep Time: 10 minutes

Cooking Time: 15 minutes

Servings: 8 persons

Ingredients
- 2 pounds frozen meatballs (Italian from Costco)
- 2 teaspoons beef base
- 8 ounces of Egg noodles
- 2 teaspoons minced garlic
- ¼ teaspoon nutmeg
- 1 ½ teaspoons onion powder
- ½ teaspoon allspice
- 1 can mushrooms (optional)
- 1 tablespoon parsley flakes
- 8 ounces' sour cream

Directions
1. Place all ingredients inside pressure cooker except sour cream. Mix well, put lid on and cook for 15 minutes on medium to high heat.
2. Remove pressure quickly, pour sour cream, and more salt and pepper if you like, stir and serve hot.

Simple Cooker Lasagne

Prep Time: 10 minutes

Cooking Time: 25 minutes

Servings: 6 persons

Ingredients

- 1 tablespoon olive oil
- 1-pound ground beef
- 1 onion, diced
- salt
- 1 24-ounce jar pasta sauce
- pepper
- 2 pounds ricotta
- ¼ cup water
- 2 large eggs
- 2 teaspoons garlic, minced
- ⅓ cup Parmesan, grated
- 1 teaspoon Italian seasoning
- 1 package mozzarella cheese, shredded
- 8 ounces lasagna noodles, no-boil variety

Directions

1. Heat the pressure cooker with oil and as it begins to smoke, add ground beef, onions, pepper, salt and cook until browned.
2. Pour water and pasta sauce to the beef mix and then transfer to a large bowl.

3. In another bowl, add eggs, ricotta, parmesan, seasoning, garlic, and pepper and salt and mix well.
4. Pour ¼ inch water in the pressure cooker once the cooker is cool.
5. Then pour a ladle of beef mix, then top with pasta, then cheese, and then repeat the same order until everything has been used. The top layer should be sauce and noodles.
6. Lock the lid and cook for 7 minutes at high heat. Then reduce heat and cook for another 7 minutes.
7. Release the stem quickly, top with more cheese and cover with lid. Let it rest for 10 minutes with no disturbance- so that the cheese melts.
8. Serve warm.

Mashed Potatoes

Prep Time: 10 minutes

Cooking Time: 10 minutes

Servings: 4 persons

Ingredients

- 1 ½ cups chicken stock
- 4 pounds red potatoes, quartered
- 1 teaspoon salt
- 1 cup heavy cream
- ½ teaspoon pepper
- 8 ounces cheddar cheese shredded
- 2 ounces butter
- 6 slices bacon, cooked and diced
- 2 tablespoons scallions
- 1 tablespoon parsley chopped

Directions

1. Heat the pressure cooker. Add stock, potatoes, salt and pepper and lock the lid.
2. Cook on high heat for 10 minutes. Then release steam slowly.
3. Pen lid, add butter, cream and all the other ingredients and stir and serve warm.

Beef Stroganoff

Prep Time: 10 minutes

Cooking Time: 30 minutes

Servings: 6 persons

Ingredients
- 3½ pounds sirloin tip roast, trimmed and cubed
- ¾ cup flour
- 2 + tablespoons olive oil
- 1 teaspoon course kosher salt
- ½ teaspoon onion powder
- ½ teaspoon pepper
- ½ teaspoon dried thyme
- ⅛ teaspoon paprika
- ½ teaspoon dried rosemary
- 1 large onion, sliced
- 1¾ cups beef stock
- 3 cloves garlic, minced
- ¼ cup red wine
- 12 ounces medium size egg noodles, cooked to package directions
- 8 ounces sour cream

Directions
1. Into a zip lock bag, add salt, pepper, flour, thyme, onion powder, rosemary, and paprika. Next add cubed meat and coat well in the flour spice mix.

2. Heat the pressure cooker with oil and add coated meat. Let it brown.
3. Transfer beef to a plate. Next add onions and sauté for 5 minutes.
4. Next add garlic and sauté until fragrant.
5. Now place beef and its cooking juices back into pan. Pour wine and beef stock and lock the lid.
6. Cook on medium heat for 20 minutes.
7. Once pressure has been released on its own, open lid,
8. Pour sour cream in a bowl.
9. Pour a small ladle of the juice from the cooker and mix into the sour cream gently and repeat until you get a loose warm liquid.
10. Pour this sour cream mix into the pressure cooker, mix, add salt and pepper and mix again.
11. To serve, arrange a plate of noodles and pour the beef stroganoff over it.

Pressure Cooked Beef Pho

Prep Time: 10 minutes

Cooking Time: 45 minutes

Servings: 8 persons

Ingredients
- 4-inch piece of ginger, sliced in half
- 2 medium yellow onions, slice in half (skin on)
- 5 pounds beef soup bones
- 6 whole cloves
- 5 whole star anise
- 1 cinnamon stick, 3 inches
- 1 tablespoon fennel seeds
- 1 tablespoon coriander seeds
- 1 black cardamom pod
- 1 ½ tablespoons salt
- 1 ounces rock sugar or regular granulated sugar
- 1-pound beef chuck, rump, brisket, cross rib roast (2×4-inch pieces)
- 4 tablespoons fish sauce

For the bowls
- ½ pound flank, eye of round, sirloin, etc., sliced thin against the grain
- 2 pounds banh pho fresh or dried rice noodles, cooked according to package directions
- 1 yellow onion, sliced thin, soaked in cold water for 30 minutes

- black pepper, ground
- 4 green onions, sliced (green part only)
- ⅓ cup cilantro, chopped
- 3 cups fresh basil (Thai basil, if you can get it)
- 2 cups fresh mint
- 2 cups mung bean sprouts
- Sriracha sauce
- 2 limes, cut into wedges
- hoisin sauce

Directions

1. For the broth, slice ginger and onions into halves. Place them on a baking sheet and broil in an oven for 10 minutes. Set aside. Remove the burnt parts.
2. Heat the pressure cooker, add beef bones, and pour water until bones are covered.
3. Place lid lightly, and boil for 5 minutes. Remove scum from bones and then pour bone into a large bowl.
4. Clean the pressure cooker, and pour 6 quarts of water and boil again. Keep removing scum as it boils.
5. Add cinnamon, anise, cloves, fennel seeds, coriander seeds, cardamom pods, salt, fish sauce, sugar and beef to the cooker.
6. Seal the lid firmly and cook on low heat for 1 hour.
7. Then allow the pressure to get released slowly. When you open the lid, strain the liquid through a mesh.

8. Now you can use this spicy broth as such. Just divide the other ingredients like noodles and raw beef slices and any other items you prefer in bowls and pour ladles of hot soup over them and enjoy.
9. If you like a less fat version of soup, place the broth in the fridge and once the fat accumulates on top, just cut it and store for later use or discard it.
10. Suppose you are not able to make the broth with 6 quarts of water, then boil with 3-4 quarts in two batches and finally mix the broth together.

Pork Pressure Ragu

Prep Time: 10 minutes

Cooking Time: 20 minutes

Servings: 6-8 persons

Ingredients

- 2 tablespoons olive oil
- 1 small yellow onion, finely diced
- 1 ½ pounds pork center loin (or pork shoulder), cut into 1-inch cubes
- 3 carrots, finely diced
- 2 cups red wine
- 4 cloves garlic, minced
- 28 ounces can whole, peeled tomatoes
- coarse salt
- 1 teaspoon good-quality dried oregano
- 1 tablespoon tomato paste
- 1 teaspoon crushed red pepper flakes

Directions

1. Heat the pressure cooker to medium high heat. Pour oil and sear the meat until brown on all sides.
2. Add the rest of the ingredients, place the lid firmly and cook fro 20 minutes.
3. Open the lid carefully once done and shred the meat with a fork.
4. Add salt and serve with polenta or pasta.

Asparagus Thyme Risotto

Prep Time: 10 minutes

Cooking Time: 10 minutes

Servings: 6 persons

Ingredients

- 2 tablespoons olive oil
- 1 cup Arborio rice
- 1 large sweet onion, coarsely chopped
- 4 garlic cloves, finely chopped
- ¼ cup fresh orange juice
- 2¾ cups vegetable stock
- 3 tablespoons fresh thyme leaves
- ½ cup grated good quality Parmesan cheese plus extra for sprinkling at the table
- 1 pound thin, fresh asparagus, cleaned and cut into 1/2 inch pieces

Directions

1. Wash the asparagus. Bend and take off the bottom part of the asparagus and discard it.
2. Sauté onions in olive oil until translucent. Add rice and coat with oil. Fry until translucent. Add garlic until fragrant.

3. Pour orange juice, stock, stir and lock the lid firmly.
4. Increase the heat and cook for 10 minutes. Open the lid slowly, add asparagus and some thyme. Place lid on for a few minutes.
5. Before serving, add cheese, stir and then serve in bowls.
6. Pass more cheese and pepper at the table.

Pork Chops in Mushroom Sauce

Prep Time: 10 minutes

Cooking Time: 10 minutes

Servings: 4 persons

Ingredients
- ½ can of water
- 1 can cream of mushroom soup
- 1 can of mushrooms
- salt and pepper to taste
- 4 pork chops

Directions
1. Add mushrooms, soup and water into the pressure cooker. Rub salt and pepper on the pork chops and place over soup mix.
2. Lick with lid and cook for 10 minutes on medium heat. The large chops, the more time.
3. Check if done to your preference and cook for more time if you like.
4. Serve with rice.

Meatballs in Tomato Gravy

Prep Time: 15 minutes

Cooking Time: 15 minutes

Servings: 4 persons

Ingredients

For the meatballs:
- ¼ cup whole milk
- ½ cup panko bread crumbs
- 3 tablespoons minced fresh parsley
- 1-ounce Parmesan cheese, grated (½ cup)
- 1-pound meatloaf mix (ground beef and pork combo
- 1 large egg (beaten)

For the sauce:
- 1 onion, minced
- 2 tablespoons olive oil
- Salt and pepper
- ¼ teaspoon red pepper flakes
- 2 tablespoons minced fresh oregano
- 6 garlic cloves, minced
- Sugar
- 2 (28-ounces) cans crushed tomatoes
- ¼ cup fresh basil (for a garnish)

Directions
1. For the sauce, heat oil in the pressure cooker.

2. Add onion and a bit salt and cook until soft.
3. Mix in oregano, 2/3rds of the garlic and red pepper flakes and cook until fragrant.
4. Pour in crushed tomatoes and stir to remove any browned bits from the bottom. Bring to simmering heat and cook until tomatoes are cooked without the raw smell.
5. Add salt, sugar and pepper and mix everything well.
6. In a bowl, pour milk and mix in panko. Then add meatloaf mix, rest of the garlic, egg, parsley, salt, pepper, Parmesan, and combine everything with your hands.
7. Shape into meatballs and place in the pressure cooker into the sauce.
8. Cook with lid locked for 5-7 minutes on low heat.
9. Once cooked, take off from heat, quickly release pressure and add salt, pepper, sugar, basil, and serve hot.

Black bean Garlic Soup

Prep Time: 30 minutes

Cooking Time: 30 minutes

Servings: 6 persons

Ingredients

- 1 pound dried black beans, soaked overnight, rinsed and drained
- 1 large red onion, chopped
- 2 tablespoons extra virgin olive oil
- 1 red bell pepper, chopped
- 1 bay leaf
- 5 garlic cloves, minced
- 2 teaspoons dried oregano
- 1 teaspoon ground cumin
- 1 teaspoon black pepper
- 2 tablespoons sherry vinegar
- 1½ teaspoon salt
- 4 cups water
- ½ cup red wine

Garnishes
- chopped tomatoes
- chopped red bell pepper
- chopped avocado
- minced scallion
- finely chopped red onion

Directions
1. Rinse the soaked beans.
2. Heat oil in a pressure cooker. Add red pepper, onions, bay leaf, cumin, garlic, oregano into the pressure cooker.
3. Sauté until fragrant for 5-8 minutes.
4. Then add beans, vinegar salt, black pepper, red wine, and water and seal the lid.
5. Cook for 15 minutes on medium to high heat.
6. Naturally release the pressure, remove lid and with the help of an immersion blender blend until everything is pureed
7. Serve in soup bowls with your preferred set of garnishes.

Beef Ribs Cooked in Cola Sauce

Prep Time: 10 minutes

Cooking Time: 10 minutes

Servings: 4 persons

Ingredients

- 2 teaspoons kosher salt
- 1 ½ teaspoons freshly ground black pepper
- 2 teaspoons paprika
- 1 ½ teaspoons cayenne pepper
- 4 to 5 pounds English-cut beef short ribs, cut crosswise into 2-1/2-inch-long pieces
- ½ teaspoon ground cumin
- 2 tablespoons olive oil
- ½ medium yellow onion, small dice
- 6 medium garlic cloves, peeled and smashed
- 2 cups cola (with sugar)
- 2 tablespoons Worcestershire sauce
- 2 tablespoons soy sauce
- 2 tablespoons water
- 2 tablespoons cornstarch

Directions

1. Mix cumin, paprika, salt, black pepper and cayenne in a bowl. Rub this mix on the ribs and keep aside.
2. Heat oil in the pressure cooker. Sear the ribs in batches and transfer to a large plate.

3. Next add garlic and onions until soft and fragrant. Pour cola, Worcestershire sauce and soy sauce into the pressure cooker and stir to release the browned bits at the bottom.
4. Place ribs back in the cooker, coat with sauce, place lid on firmly, and cook on medium high for 30 minutes.
5. Naturally release the steam once the time is over.
6. Then open the cooker carefully.
7. Keep a large bowl and place a strainer over it.
8. Gently take out the ribs and place on a plate.
9. Pour juice into strainer and then pour this clear juice back into cooker.
10. Boil over high heat. Meanwhile mix corn starch with a little water and pour this mix into boiling liquid.
11. Once it thickens, pour this sauce over ribs and serve hot.

Desserts

Peach Cobbler

Prep Time: 10 minutes

Cooking Time: 10 minutes

Servings: 6-8 persons

Ingredients

Peach Filling:
- ¼ cup sugar
- 12 fresh peaches, peeled, pitted, and sliced into 1" wedges
- ¼ cup brown sugar
- 2 teaspoons lemon juice
- ¼ teaspoon cinnamon
- ¾ cup water
- 3 tablespoons cornstarch

Topping:
- ½ cup milk
- 2⅓ cup baking mix
- 3 tablespoons butter, melted
- 4½ tablespoons sugar, divided
- 1 teaspoon vanilla

- ½ teaspoon cinnamon

Directions

1. For the peach filling: mix into a bowl some sugar, peaches, cinnamon, brown sugar, corn starch, lemon juice, water and pour it all into a pressure cooker.
2. For the topping: into a bowl, add butter, baking mix, vanilla, milk and 3 tablespoons of sugar and mix well. In a separate bowl, add cinnamon and the rest of the sugar and mix well.
3. Into the pressure cooker, sprinkle topping mix over peach mix and then sprinkle cinnamon sugar mix onto the topping.
4. Lock the lid securely and cook on high heat for 10 minutes, then release pressure naturally and then open and enjoy warm.

Apple Crumble Cooker Cake

Prep Time: 10 minutes

Cooking Time: 10 minutes

Servings: 4 persons

Ingredients

- 11 tablespoons melted butter
- 6 small apples (red or yellow)
- 3 tablespoons soft butter
- 10 dry bread crumbs
- 8 sugar
- 1 teaspoon ginger powder
- 2 tablespoons flour
- half a lemon
- 1 teaspoon cinnamon

Directions

1. Choose a baking pan to fit inside the steamer basket of the pressure cooker first.
2. Mix the sugar, ginger, breadcrumbs, melted butter, cinnamon and lemon juice and zest in a bowl to make the crumb mix.
3. Core and wash the apples. Slice them thinly.
4. Spread butter on a baking pan and then dust with flour.

5. Arrange apple slices in concentric circles neatly in one layer. Top with the crumb mix.
6. If you have more apples, add one layer of apples and then top again with crumb mix.
7. Cover the pan with foil paper.
8. Pour 2 cups of water into the pressure cooker and place the steamer basket into the pressure cooker.
9. Place the baking pan inside the steamer, switch on the stove and close the pressure cooker's lid firmly.
10. Cook for 20 minutes on high heat and let the pressure get released naturally.
11. Let the crumble rest for 10-15 minutes, let it be a warm to cool temperature and then take out.
12. Once you take out, sprinkle raw sugar on top of cake and then broil in the oven for 2 minutes just to caramelize the sugar. Then slice and serve.

40 Minute Dulce De Leche

Prep Time: 5 minutes

Cooking Time: 40 minutes

Servings: 2-4 persons

Ingredients

- 1 can of sweetened, condensed milk

Directions

1. Take the can of condensed sweet milk and place into the pressure cooker.
2. Pour water just to cover the can in the pressure cooker.
3. Keep the can to a side, or else it will bounce once the water begins to boil.
4. Place the lid firmly and cook on medium to high heat for about 35-40 minutes.
5. Then release the pressure carefully and slowly. Take out the very hot can with tongs and some thick cloth and let it cool to room temperature.
6. Open it and enjoy thick creamy dulce de leche. If it gets too sticky, just soften it in the double broiler before serving. Store the rest in the refrigerator.
7. Use as a topping on ice cream, cookies and other desserts.

Walnut Banana Cake

Prep Time: 15 minutes

Cooking Time: 50 minutes

Servings: 4-8 persons/makes 2 small cakes

Ingredients
- 1 egg
- 2 ripe bananas, chopped
- 6 tablespoons + 2 tablespoons all purpose flour
- 5 tablespoons sugar
- 1 ½ tablespoons walnuts
- ¼ teaspoon salt
- butter or ghee - for greasing the cake molds
- ¼ teaspoon vanilla

Directions
1. Heat the pressure cooker at a low flame. Place a base plate at the bottom of the cooker. Close the lid and let it heat up for 10 minutes. This is the preheating process.
2. Chop walnuts and dust with flour and keep aside.
3. Blend in a blender the rest of the ingredients and pour into a bowl. Finally, walnuts and mix.
4. Grease 2 cake molds with ghee and pour the batter into it, just filling until ¾ full.

5. Place each one carefully in the pressure cooker and bake for 40 minutes with lid on but do not put on the whistle. You can bake only one at a time.
6. Open the lid; insert a toothpick to check it comes out dry.
7. Leave to cool for 10 minutes, then cut and serve.
8. If you have a large pressure cooker, then opt for a larger baking pan and pour the batter at one go (but not to the brim) and bake.

Decadent Chocolate Cheesecake

Prep Time: 30 minutes

Cooking Time: 30 minutes

Servings: 6-8 persons

Ingredients

For the Crumb Crust
- 4 tablespoons melted butter
- 1½ cups cookie crumbs (chocolate, preferably. If you don't have chocolate wafers or cookies, use graham crackers or vanilla wafers and add 1½ tablespoons cocoa powder)

For the Cheesecake Batter
- 5 ounces brown sugar, sifted to remove any lumps (about⅔ cup, sifted and firmly packed)
- 1 pound (2 8 ounces blocks) cream cheese at room temperature
- 1 teaspoon vanilla paste or extract
- 2 ounces sour cream, whipping cream or buttermilk at room temperature
- 6 ounces bittersweet chocolate, melted and cooled to just warm
- 1½ teaspoons instant coffee dissolved in 1½ teaspoons water
- 2 Tablespoons cocoa powder

For the Topping

- 1 ounce each dark chocolate, melted
- 1-ounce milk chocolate, melted
- 1-ounce white chocolate, melted

Directions

1. Grease a spring form pan with spray. Line with parchment paper.
2. Mix butter and cookie crumbs until they hold onto together when you press a little of the mix in your palms.
3. Press this mix evenly into the pan.
4. Bake at 350F for 10 minutes. Leave aside to cool.
5. The cheesecake batter: preheat a large cake pan that can hold a 6-inch pan with a 2-inch clearance all around it.
6. Pour water - about 2 quarts into the large pan and leave to boil in the oven.
7. Beat cream cheese until smooth. Crack eggs and mix into cheese. Scrap the sides as you mix.
8. Mix in cocoa powder, sour cream in a separate bowl and then pour into the cheese bowl and incorporate everything gently.
9. Pour on top of baked crust and place in the boiling water in the large pan in the oven.
10. Bake for 45- 55 minutes until the cheesecake is set and not jelly like any more.
11. Once done, remove from water bath, let it cool to room temperature and then place in refrigerator to completely set and cool.

12. For the topping, melt chocolate and drizzle in any style you like over the cheesecake.

Lava Cake

Prep Time: 10 minutes

Cooking Time: 10 minutes

Servings: 4 persons

Ingredients

- ¼ cup powder sugar
- ½ cup semi-sweet chocolate chips
- 2 tablespoons all-purpose-flour
- 1 egg
- 4 tablespoons butter
- 1 teaspoon vanilla

Directions

1. Make sure that butter is at room temperature. Also take a cake pan that can fit inside the pressure cooker.
2. Grease the cake mold with butter. You can use any baking dish or microwave safe dish, but not glass.
3. Place a base plate at the bottom of the cooker so that the cake pan can be kept on top of it. Pour 2 cups of water onto this base plate.
4. Sift sugar ad flour and keep aside.

5. Melt butter and chocolate chips in the microwave for 30 seconds. Mix and keep aside.
6. Beat egg and vanilla into the butter mix.
7. Finally, flour sugar mix into the butter and egg mix and stir with a spoon.
8. Pour into cake pan and place into the pressure cooker.
9. Latch the lid on and cook on high heat for 7 minutes.
10. Take the cake pan, and let it cool. Then take out of pan and serve in slices.

Rice Pudding

Prep Time: 10 minutes

Cooking Time: 10 minutes

Servings: 4-7 persons

Ingredients

- 1¾ cups water
- 1 cup white rice
- ¼ teaspoon salt
- ⅓ cup sugar
- 2 cups milk
- 2 eggs
- ¼ teaspoon cinnamon
- 1 teaspoon vanilla extract
- ¾ cup raisins

Directions

1. Take the pressure cooker, water, rice and salt and put on the lid firmly.
2. Cook for 5 minutes on high heat.
3. Release the steam quickly and open the lid.
4. Pour 1.5 cups of milk and sugar and combine well.
5. In a bowl, beat eggs with the rest of the milk, cinnamon and vanilla and mix well. Take small spoonfuls of rice mix and add to the egg mix to warm it evenly.

6. Once it is arm enough, pour the egg mix into the pressure cooker and whisk quickly.
7. Place pressure cooker back on medium heat and boil it for 5 minutes.
8. Then take off heat, add raisins, stir and serve warm or cold.

Chocolate Mousse

Prep Time: 10 minutes

Cooking Time: 25 minutes

Servings: 4-6 persons

Ingredients

- 1 cup full-cream milk
- 1 ¼ cups pouring cream
- ¼ cup caster sugar
- 6 egg yolks
- 1 ¼ cups dark cooking chocolate, broken into chunks
- 1 teaspoon vanilla extract
- fresh raspberries, to serve (optional)
- sifted cocoa, for dusting

Directions

1. Grease a baking dish that can fit inside the pressure cooker.
2. In a saucepan, add milk, cream and sugar and simmer it at a low heat until sugar has been dissolved. Take off from heat.
3. Add chocolate pieces to this cream mix and stir until melted.
4. Beat eggs in a bowl, and pour into chocolate mix in the saucepan. Pour vanilla and mix again.
5. Pour into baking dish and cover with foil.

6. Place a base plate or trivet at the bottom of the pressure cooker and pour 2 cups water.
7. Place the baking dish on top of base plate. Lock the lid properly and cook at low heat for 25 minutes.
8. Once done, release pressure naturally, and take out the mousse carefully.
9. Leave to cool and then chill in the fridge before serving.
10. Serve with fresh raspberries and cocoa powder dusting.

Carrot Halva

Prep Time: 10 minutes

Cooking Time: 7 minutes

Servings: 4-8 persons

Ingredients

- 1 cup milk
- 4 cups grated carrots
- 1 ½ cups sugar
- 10 cashew nuts
- 3 tablespoons ghee or clarified butter
- 2 tablespoons raisins
- 4 tablespoons milk powder
- ¼ teaspoon cardamom, ground

Directions

1. Peel and wash carrots. Grate them in a food processor or with a grater.
2. Heat ghee in a pressure cooker, add raisins and fry until puffed for seconds. Take put and keep aside. Fry cashew nuts until golden brown and kept aside.
3. Pour 1 teaspoon of ghee, fry the grated carrots for 5 minutes on medium heat. Pour milk and stir. Close lid and cook on high heat for 1 whistle.
4. Once the pressure gets released, open lid and check if milk has been absorbed or else boils it for 5 minutes until milk is absorbed.

5. Add sugar and stir on a medium flame until the mix gets sticky and the sugar should have melted.
6. Add milk powder at this point and stir for 10 seconds.
7. Finally add cardamom powder, cashew nuts and raisins, mix and cook for 1 minute and serve hot.

Blueberry Delight

Prep Time: 10 minutes

Cooking Time: 35 minutes

Servings: 4-7 persons

Ingredients

- 1 ½ teaspoon baking powder
- 1 cup plain flour
- ½ teaspoon salt
- 2 ½ tablespoons dried breadcrumbs
- ½ cup butter, cut into small pieces, plus extra for greasing
- ½ cup granulated sugar
- 5 ounces milk
- 1 egg, beaten
- Crème fraîche or cream, to serve
- ½ pound blueberries

Directions

1. Grease a pudding dish and keep aside.
2. Sift baking powder, flour and salt in a bowl. Add butter cubes, breadcrumbs and sugar into flour and mix well.
3. Next add milk and eggs and stir well.
4. Finally add in blueberries, stir and pour into dish filling only up to ¾ full.

5. Heat a pressure cooker, place base plate, pour 2 cups water and boil it.
6. Place a steamer basket in the pressure cooker and place the pudding dish into the steamer.
7. Close lid firmly and cook on high heat for 35 minutes.
8. Quickly release steam, take out the blueberry delight carefully and turn out on a large plate. Serve with cream of you like.

Part 2

Have You Heard Of The Instant Pot?

I'm sure you've heard of the Instant pot by now. It's been the hot new cooking appliance for the past few months. Chances are that you've seen it on the shelves of your local superstore, on Amazon, or maybe you've come across one of the many blog posts, social media posts, or forum posts singing the praises of this fresh take on the old-fashioned pressure cooker.

I've always been intrigued by the idea of a pressure cooker, but to be perfectly honest, it's always scared me. The Instant Pot is the perfect solution for people like me, who like the idea of cooking a tender roast in a fraction of the time that it takes in the oven or slow cooker.

While our mothers and grandmothers were comfortable using a stovetop pressure cooker, most women of this generation have been intimidated by the hissing and the potential of having it blow up. Because of this, pressure cooking has fallen out of favor in the last few decades. All that has changed with the arrival of the Instant Pot - a self-contained, electrical pressure cooker with plenty of built in safety features.

With the promise of being able to cook a meal in 3 to 10 minutes of pressure cooking, it is no surprise that this new electric appliance is quickly gaining a large fan base. Instant Pots are flying off the shelves, and you can find plenty of fans online who share their favorite recipes, tips, and adaptations on blogs and popular Instant Pot Facebook groups.

The instant pot is a self-contained unit that sits on your counter top and plugs into an outlet. It takes up about as much space as a rice cooker or a small slow cooker. The Instant Pot is a smart pressure cooker that's controlled through a digital interface. You tell it how long you want to cook your meal under pressure, set the timer and you're good to go. It automatically brings up and holds the pressure at a safe level and will not allow you to open the pot while it's pressurized. This makes it as easy to operate as a microwave.

It is not surprising then that this new take on an old kitchen tool is quickly gaining popularity. The cooking is very hands-off. You simply set it, and then walk away until you're food is ready. It has all the advantages of using the slow cooker, but takes a fraction of the time. Perfect when you want to get a home cooked meal on the table fast.

Does The Instant Pot Really Cook That Fast?

One of the big appeals of the Instant pot when you first start to look at it is how quickly it claims to cook food. I know it's what first attracted me to this new kitchen appliance. Being able to cook an entire Sunday dinner in 15 minutes or less sounded very appealing, but also a little too good to be true Let's take a closer look at how fast the Instant Pot actually cooks your food.

Let me start by pointing out that it does indeed cook pretty fast. It really shines on dishes like stews or roasts that would otherwise take a long time on the stove or in the oven, and even longer in the slow cooker.

Truth be told, the claims that it can cook chicken breast in 5 minutes, or a roast in 20 minutes, are a little misleading. While that is the time the food needs to cook under pressure, the actual time before you can eat is longer because it has to come up to pressure first. This process can take anywhere from ten minutes to half an hour. The fuller the pot, the colder (or even frozen) the ingredients, and the bigger the cut of meat, the longer it will take to come up to pressure. Once it does, the countdown timer will start.

After the food has cooked for the allotted time, it takes a little while before you can safely open the pot and serve your meal. There are two options and which one you choose depends on the meal you're preparing. The first is to release the pressure through the vent in the lid. This causes hot steam to escape and the pressure to go down within a matter of minutes. Once that's done, you'll be able to open the lid and serve the food.

The second option is a process called Natural Pressure Release (NPR). Whenever a recipe calls for this, you shouldn't turn the valve to release the pressure. Instead, you let the pot sit until the pressure releases on its own. This process takes about 25 to 45 minutes and allows the food to continue cooking, until the pressure valve drops down and you are able to open the pot... It's important to allow for this additional time when preparing a meal in the Instant Pot.

All in all, you won't be able to cook your meals in a matter of minutes. You have to figure in the time it will take for the pot to come up to pressure, and for some recipes, additional time to allow the pressure to slowly drop back down. Does this mean the Instant Pot isn't fast? Of course not. It's still a much quicker method of cooking roasts, beans and the likes than any other cooking style. In short it's not super-fast for everything, but great for things that take a long time otherwise.

As an added bonus, once you add everything to the pot, it is hands-free cooking. You don't have to stir pots or babysit the food. Instead, you can work on something else, or relax for a bit while dinner cooks itself.

How To Choose The Right Instant Pot

You've heard about the Instant Pot and are ready to buy one and give this modern take on pressure cooking a try. You head to the store or your favorite online store and discover that there are quite a few different models of Instant Pot available, in different sizes, with different functionality. Let me quickly run you through the most popular models and sizes so you can make an informed decision on what to get.

Let's start by talking about size. The size of meals you want to cook, or even the size of your family will determine what Instant Pot is the right size for you. Most come in the following sizes:

- 5 Quart
- 6 Quart
- 8 Quart

The 5 quart size works well if you're mainly cooking for one to three people. It works great for dorm rooms, and is a must have in a small apartment. Unless that description fits you, I highly recommend going with the standard 6 quart size.

The six quart model is the most versatile and also the most popular size. Some of the models available will only come in this size. It's perfect for the average family and will fit all your pressure cooking needs. If in doubt, go with this size.

The 8 quart size is available in a few models and is a good fit for larger families, or if you know you'll be cooking a lot of large meals for family gatherings, church dinners and such.

With size decisions out of the way, let's take a quick look at the different models available. There are three different main models with a couple of variations thrown in to keep you on your toes. Here are the main models.

The Instant Pot Lux

This is the basic Instant Pot model and the one I recommend for most people new to pressure cooking. You may also hear as this one as the 6-in-1 model. It's a pressure cooker, slow cooker, steamer, rice cooker, with sauté and keep warm functions as well for a total of six different ways of cooking.

The Instant Pot Duo

This is also called the 7-in-1 and will do everything the Lux can, but is also a yogurt maker. If making your own yogurt at home is on your list of things you want to do regularly, spring for the duo, otherwise, go with the basic lux model and save a few dollars.

The Instant Pot Smart + app

The latest main model in the Instant Pot lineup is the Smart one. It will do everything the previous two models do and more. The digital interface on the pot itself and the app that connects to your instant pot, allow you to control temperature and cooking durations for your meals as you see fit.

If you like gadgets, prefer the ease of being able to save your favorite recipes and instant pot settings on your smart phone, and love full control over your pot, this is the model to get.

If you're on a budget, go for the Lux model. If you're a big fan of making yogurt, consider the Duo, and if your budget allows, go for the latest model with full smartphone app integration. To be perfectly honest, it's hard to go wrong no matter what model of instant pot you choose.

Is An Instant Pot Worth The Money?

Let's take a look at the instant pot and whether or not it's worth spending the money on one. Depending on the time of year, and what kind of deal you can find, the average Instant Pot will set you back anywhere from $70 to $150. While this doesn't make it the cheapest kitchen appliance on the market, it's also nowhere near the highest.

On the other hand you can pick up a stovetop pressure cooker or basic slow cooker for around $25. Does that mean the Instant Pot is overpriced, or something you shouldn't consider buying? I don't think so. While the Instant Pot may not be the right choice for everyone, it can quickly become one of your most valued and most often used appliances.

For example, the inexpensive stove top pressure cooker will do you no good if you're too intimidated to use it, or end up keeping it in the back of the cabinet because you don't have the time and patience to keep an eye on the pressure and adjust the stovetop as needed. If you have young children underfoot, you may not be comfortable using a traditional pressure cooker so the Instant Pot provides a great alternative.

If you're good at planning ahead and starting dinner first thing in the morning to slow cook a roast, you may not need an Instant Pot. If on the other hand, you're like me and forget to get it started, the Instant Pot may just be the solution you need to get dinner on the table quickly.

Last but not least, let's talk hard cash. The expense of buying the Instant Pot will easily be worth it, if it keeps you from going out to eat, or picking up food on your way home. If you know you can get dinner cooked in 45 minutes without having to stir pots, it becomes a lot easier to go home and start that pot of chili, or the pot roast, and relax while it cooks. If it keeps you from ordering out even just once a week, it won't be long for the Instant Pot to pay for itself.

At the end of the day, the decision is yours to make. If you aren't sure if you'll actually use it, the Instant Pot may be a waste of money. If on the other hand, you think you'll use it quite a bit then keep it on your counter and use it as your pressure cooker, slow cooker, and rice cooker, it will be an investment that's well worth it. Look through some recipes, borrow a friend's Instant Pot if possible, and see if this seems like the type of appliance that will work well for you and your lifestyle.

Instant Pot vs. Slowcooker

When you start to look into the benefits of using an Instant Pot, you may notice that there's quite a bit of overlap with the benefits of using a slow cooker. Both appliances are good at cooking large, inexpensive cuts of meat like pork and beef roasts for example. Both are great at cooking beans, soups, stews, chilies and the likes. Both are also great for busy home cooks, since they allow you put everything in, turn it on, and let the food cook itself. No stirring pots and watching the stove required.

In addition, both are electric appliances that sit on your counter top and plug into an available outlet. You can move them around as needed, they use up approximately the same amount of space, and you can take them with you to family get-togethers, vacations etc. They even both excel at keeping food piping hot until you're ready to eat.

The biggest difference between the Instant Pot and the Slow Cooker is cooking time. The slow cooker is designed to cook your meal low and slow. The average slow cooker dish takes six to ten hours to cook. The instant pot on the other hand will cook most meals in under an hour from start to finish.

Another big difference is that while a slow cooker is just that, a device that cooks your meals low and slow, the Instant Pot can replace your rice cooker as well as your slow cooker since it has a slow cooker setting. Depending on the model you choose, you can even replace your yogurt maker with it.

If you want more versatility in one appliance and the ability to cook a wholesome home cooked meal in a very short time, the Instant Pot is the way to go. I encourage you to give it a try and see if it becomes one of the most used kitchen appliances in your house like it has in mine.

If on the other hand you are comfortable with your slow cooker and good about planning ahead long enough to start your dinner in it, you may find that you have no need for an Instant Pot. Similarly, if you think the hissing and steaming, or simply the idea of having a pressure cooking device in your kitchen scares you then you're probably better off sticking to your slow cooker. That being said, with the safety features built in and the easy to use digital display, using an instant pot is just as simple and easy as your favorite slow cooker. If you're feeling a little intimidated, I encourage you to get one and give it a try. After preparing your first two or three meals in it, you'll be wondering what you were worried about in the first place.

Breakfast, Lunch, And Dinner In The Instant Pot

One of my favorite things about the Instant Pot is how versatile it is. You can cook a wide variety of dishes in this popular new electric appliance. In this post, we're going to take a quick look at how you can cook breakfast, lunch, and dinner in this electric pressure cooker. This will come in handy when your stove is out, it's too hot to cook inside, you're on vacation, or when you're cooking with your Instant Pot in your dorm room for example.

Of course these aren't the only times the versatility of the Instant pot will come in handy. I like to use my Instant Pot multiple times per week and cook a wide variety of dishes in it for any time of the day. Let' me quickly run you through some family favorites for breakfast, lunch, and dinner.

Breakfast In The Instant Pot

Let's start with the first meal of the day – breakfast. There are all sorts of great dishes you can make in the Instant Pot. With the sauté function, you can even use it to scramble up some eggs or cook sausage in a pinch.

Where the Instant Pot really shines is with oatmeal. Some of the best tasting steel cut oats come from cooking them in this popular electric appliance. No constant stirring required for creamy and nutritious oats.

You can even hard boil a large quantity of eggs in your Instant Pot. Perfect for make ahead breakfast meals that last you all week long.

Lunch In The Instant Pot

Since the Instant Pot does such a great job at fixing soups and stews, it's perfect for lunchtime cooking as well. With a quick google search you'll be able to find plenty of yummy recipes to try as well as lots of directions for adapting your own favorite recipes.

It's also a great way to cook one pot meals including pasta and rice dishes that are perfect for lunch. And let's not forget about everyone's favorite – Mac and Cheese. If on the other hand you're in the mood for a nice salad, try boiling eggs for it in the instant pot, or even making an entire batch of potato salad in it from start to finish.

Dinner In The Instant Pot

Last but not least, let's talk about dinner. This is where the Instant pot really shines. It's great for easy weeknight dinners that can be cooked from start to finish in the instant pot like a nice big batch of beef stew, or your favorite chicken dish for example.

Pressure cookers have always been the best way to deal with large roasts and tougher cuts of meat. Cook your pot roast or a big batch of homemade pulled pork in the slow cooker for a nice Sunday dinner.

And let's not forget about side dishes. From various rice dishes to mashed, or scalloped potatoes, the instant pot can take care of your main side dish for you while you're busy cooking anything else.

Unusual Ways To Use Your Instant Pot

Some fun and unusual stuff you can do. I.e. make vanilla extract, cheese cake, and can in the instant pot

So you have an Instant Pot and you've been using it regularly to cook all the typical pressure cooker dishes. You put it to good use for your Sunday roast, whip up a quick last minute dinner during the week, and even cook oatmeal in it a few times per week for breakfast. In short, the Instant Pot has become a staple appliance in your home.

Then you start to wonder what else this electric pressure cooker can do. I'm here with some fun ideas for unusual ways to make the most from your Instant Pot. While these may not be the things you will be making on a weekly or even monthly basis, they are fun to try and have their good uses.

Bake A Cheese Cake

The Instant Pot makes some of the yummiest and easiest cheese cakes. Yes, that's right. You can sort of bake in your instant pot. You'll need a spring form that fits inside your instant pot, a rack for the baking pan to sit in and of course a delicious cheese cake recipe.

A quick search will bring up an almost endless supply of yummy recipes to try. Pick one and start stirring your pot. Before long you'll be making one of your favorite indulged desserts in the Instant Pot. This is perfect for when you want to impress your guests or bring something unusual to the office pot luck.

Can Some Jam

Traditional pressure cookers are great for canning all sorts of fruits and vegetables. While the Instant Pot wasn't designed with canning and food preservation in mind, you can do a little small batch canning in it.

This is perfect if you want to turn some of those ripe fruits from the local farmers market into some artisan jam. Use the Instant Pot to preserve and pressure seal your jars. Since you're processing in small batches, you can try out various different and fun recipes and end up with some delicious jams and preserves to enjoy throughout the year.

Make Homemade Vanilla Extract

Do you use vanilla extract in your cooking and baking? I go through quite a bit, particularly during the holiday season. There's nothing quite like real vanilla extract, but let's be honest, it's outrageously pricey. Why not make your own homemade vanilla extract in your Instant Pot?

That's right… you can make your own homemade version using real vanilla beans and vodka or other high spirit. Not only is it some of the best tasting extract you'll ever use, it's also a wonderful gift to give to loved ones.

The Instant Pot Saves Time And Money

We're all busy and spending less and less time at home. As a result, it's hard to find the time to cook a nice home cooked meal. We simply can't spend hours and hours in the kitchen stirring pots. Heck most of us don't even have the time or energy at the end of the day for a quick 30 minute meal cooked from scratch.

The end result is that we rely on convenience food and takeout. While those options certainly save a good bit of time, we end up paying a lot more for our food. Let's not even mention the fact that it isn't always the healthiest food out there and we're not sure what ingredients and preservatives are in the food.

What if there was a way to save both time and money, and still get wholesome, home cooked meals on those nights when you don't have a lot of time or energy left. There is and the solution to your problem is the Instant Pot. Not only does it cook your food faster than just about any other method of cooking, it is also very hands-free. You can even cook frozen meat and veggies for those days when you forget to thaw ahead of time.

This means that you can come home, throw some ingredients in the Instant Pot, turn it on, and then focus your attention on something else. This means that you can help your kids with homework, start a load of laundry, catch up on work email, or just sit back and relax for half an hour before dinner is served.

In other words, the Instant Pot saves you time in two different ways. It will take less time overall to cook the food, and most of the cooking time doesn't require you to be there, stirring pots and playing an active role in the cooking process. That's a big deal and something you'll come to appreciate when you start to use your Instant Pot regularly.

Now it's time to talk hard, cold cash. An Instant Pot is a bit of an investment, even when you can find a great "Black Friday" style deal on it. On average, you can expect to spend about $100 for this electric pressure cooker. The good news is that it won't take you long to recoup this investment.

An instant pot allows you to cook more at home instead of going out to eat, or ordering takeout. This alone will save you anywhere from $5 to $50 per family meal. But it doesn't stop there. The Instant Pot really shines with inexpensive cuts of meat like roasts, whole chickens and even more frugal fare like beans and rice. If you get in the habit of making just one frugal meal per week using your pressure cooker, those savings will quickly add up.

You can go even further by cooking double batches and taking leftovers for lunch instead of buying it. Saving time and money with an Instant Pot is quick, easy, and almost automatic. The only trick is that you have to actually get in the habit of using it regularly.

Is The Instant Pot Safe?

Pressure cookers have been around for a long time, and just as long have the incidents of them exploding in the kitchen due to user error. While they are a great cooking tool and most of us can remember a grandmother, aunt, or other relative having one and cooking with it regularly, most of us in this day and age have been more than a little bit intimidated by the regular stove top models.

I can't say I blame you, if you feel the same. We're in the same boat. While I love the idea of being able to cook food quickly and in a healthy way by cooking it under pressure, I have never been comfortable being in the same room with one, not to mention actually using it. The hissing, steaming, and rattling alone is enough to send the bravest of home cooks to the hills.

Thankfully there's a new pressure cooker kid on the block – the Instant Pot and it's much safer and more convenient to use than the standard stove top models. It has a total of 10 built in safety features that will keep you and your loved ones safe and secure. Combined they ensure that it is almost impossible to go wrong due to user error or equipment failure.

Let's take the locking mechanism as an example. With a regular stove-top pressure cooker, it's easy to try to lift the lid while the container is still under pressure and burn yourself with the hot steam that will escape violently. The Instant Pot lid will not open until the pressure is back to normal.

Automatic pressure control and pressure regulators keep the pressure in the pot under control. This means you can't generate the kind of pressure inside your pot that could cause it to explode all over your kitchen. If you ask me, that's a very good thing.

It even has sensors built in that keep temperature in check and keep you from burning you food in cases where there isn't enough liquid in the pot to build up the appropriate cooking pressure. Instead of continuing to heat on high and burning the food inside the pressure cooker, it simply switches to the keep warm function, allowing you to add liquid and start over.

You can check the Instant Pot website for full details on all 10 safety features of the Instant Pot and how they make pressure cooking safer than ever. As long as you make sure the device isn't damaged and keep the sealing ring, lid, and vent clean, cooking in this smart new appliance is as safe as anything else you do in the kitchen.

Yes, there's still a bit of hissing steam before your cooker hits full pressure and the safety valve closes, but that just makes it fun and exciting. After the first few times of using your Instant Pot, you won't even think twice about it. Give it a try. I think you'll love this fast new way to cook healthy, homemade meals.

How To Find Instant Pot Recipes

You bought an Instant Pot, brought it home, and got it set up. You did your water test, boiled some eggs in it, and maybe even made a handful of dishes from recipes on the Instant Pot website or in the included recipe guide. Now that you're comfortable using this new electric appliance, you're ready to branch out and start to look for some other fun recipes to try. Here are some of the best places both online and offline to find Instant Pot Recipes.

Go Old School With Cookbooks And Recipes Cards

Since the Instant Pot has been so popular for the past few months, there are plenty of traditional cookbooks (along with eBook versions) being published. Browse through your local bookstore, or head on over to Amazon.com to see what's available right now.

If you have friends or family members who are Instant Pot fans, ask them for their favorite recipes and jot them down on recipe cards. If there's a group of you, you can start to regularly exchange recipes. If someone brings an Instant Pot dish to a potluck or gathering, ask them for the recipe. It won't take you long to establish a nice little library of tried and true recipes.

Blogs And Google Searches

If you're looking for something specific, doing a quick Google search is always a great idea. You'll be able to find chicken thigh specific recipes, or instant pot ready recipes for spaghetti and meatballs.

Along the way, you'll likely come across all sorts of different blogs where fellow Instant Pot users share their experiences and recipes. Bookmark them, or simply browse around when you come across them for plenty of fresh recipe ideas. Try the recipes as is, or use them as inspiration to come up with your own take on a dish.

Go Social With Pinterest And Facebook Groups

Last but not least, let's not forget about social media. Pinterest is a great source of Instant Pot recipes. Do a quick search and follow a few Instant Pot or Pressure Cooker boards for plenty of new recipe ideas in your Pinterest Feed.

By far my favorite way to come across new recipes to try or get suggestions for recipe adaptations, is Facebook groups. There are several good Instant Pot specific groups you can join and participate in. You'll find a wealth of information in these groups along with all sorts of helpful tips and ideas.

With these suggestions, I'm sure you'll find more Instant Pot recipes than you'd ever get a chance to try. Cook up the ones that look good or sound delicious and start to build up your very own library of family favorite Instant Pot recipes.

All recipes are written to serve 4-6

Stuffed Peppers

Ingredients
4 large green peppers (cut and deseeded)
1 lb. ground lean beef or turkey
½ tsp salt
¼ tsp black pepper
1 medium onion (diced)
1 can french onion soup
2 x ¼ cup water
1 ½ cups uncooked rice
1 tbsp. coconut oil (or any cooking oil)

Instructions
1. Set your pressure cooker to Sauté mode.
2. When cooker is hot, add oil to pot, and then add diced onions. Sauté onions until brown and caramelized.
3. Add ground meat, salt and pepper. Brown meat, breaking it into small pieces.
4. Add a french onion soup, rice and water. Mix. There'll be some liquid from the meat already. Be careful not to add too much water to the mixture so the rice won't get too wet.
5. Cancel sauté mode. Cover cooker, making sure to lock the lid. Set steam release to seal.
6. Set cooker to high pressure for 8 minutes.

7. Quick release after cooking is done. Stir rice & meat mixture.
8. Stuff green peppers with mixture.
9. Remove extra mixture from cooker. Add about ¼ cup water to cooker.
10. Return stuffed peppers to cooker, set cooker to steam or 4 minutes on high pressure.
11. Quick or natural release after cooking time.
12. Serve hot.

Spaghetti And Meatballs

Ingredients

2 lbs. ground beef or turkey
1 tsp chopped garlic or garlic powder
1 tsp onion powder
1 tsp salt (or less if you prefer)
¼ tsp paprika
¼ tsp oregano
1 egg
½ lb. dry, uncooked spaghetti
1 jar 67oz spaghetti sauce
1 tbsp. cooking oil
½ tsp chopped garlic
Water

Instructions

1. Mix ground meat, dry seasoning and egg well. Use a small ice cream scoop to make evenly sized meatballs.
2. Set pressure cooker to sauté mode. Once hot, add oil and garlic.
3. Add meatballs in one layer. Turn over meatballs to brown evenly. Remove meatballs. Set aside. Continue working in batches until all meatballs are browned. Note: They don't have to be fully cooked as they will be cooked further later on.
4. Add water to cooker, scraping bottom to release browned bits. Add about ½ cup of spaghetti sauce to the water. Mix well.

5. Add uncooked spaghetti to pot. Add water until spaghetti is covered. Cook on high pressure at 4-5 minutes.
6. Quick release, remove cooked spaghetti from cooker. Return meatballs to pot, add rest of spaghetti sauce. Cook on high pressure for another 8 minutes.
7. Natural release. Serve meatballs, sauce on spaghetti. Garnish with Parmesan cheese if you wish.

Quick Shredded Buffalo Chicken Sandwiches

Ingredients

4 pieces chicken breasts
1 envelope dry ranch seasoning or 2 tbsp. homemade ranch seasoning
½ cup or more buffalo sauce - any
Hamburger buns or flatbread

Instructions

1. Place chicken breasts in pressure cooker. Sprinkle seasoning over chicken. Cook on high pressure for 10 minutes. Quick release.
2. Shred chicken with fork. Tip: Use a hand mixer for quick and easy shredding.
3. Pour buffalo sauce over chicken. Mix well. Add more if you prefer a spicy and saucy filling.
4. Serve hot on hamburger buns or on flat bread.

One Pot Creamy Chicken & Rice

Ingredients
1 tbsp. cooking oil
2 piece chicken breast cut into bite sized chunks
1 tsp chopped garlic
1 tsp salt
¼ tsp black pepper
1 cup uncooked rice (washed)
1 cup chicken broth (or 1 tsp chicken base + 1 cup water)
½ cup heavy cream
2 cups green beans

Instructions
1. Set pressure cooker to sauté mode. Once hot, heat cooking oil. Add garlic, salt, pepper and cut chicken. Stir until chicken is about half cooked.
2. Add uncooked rice, chicken broth. Mix well. Cover and set pressure cooker to cook on high pressure for 8 - 10 minutes. Allow longer if using brown rice.
3. Quick release. Add cream, stir.
4. Add green beans. Cover and cook on high pressure for another 2 minutes.
5. Quick release, serve hot.

Quick Leftover Chicken Pizza

Ingredients
¾ cup spaghetti sauce
4 pieces frozen leftover (cooked) chicken
1 tube refrigerated pizza dough
1 cup shredded mozzarella cheese

Instructions
1. Spread spaghetti sauce inside cooker pot. Place chicken breasts on top of sauce. Set pressure cooker to high for 10 minutes.
2. While chicken is cooking, heat oven to 350F, lay out pizza dough on pan.
3. Quick release, shred chicken.
4. Spread chicken evenly over dough. Sprinkle cheese over top of chicken. Bake at 350% for 10-12 minutes or following instructions for dough or until crust is crisp and browned

Easy Peasy Roast

Ingredients
1 medium onion sliced
1 tbsp. oil
2 lb. rump roast (or your preferred cut)
¼ cup water
1 packet Au Jus gravy mix
1 packet Dry Ranch Dressing
1 tbsp. corn starch mixed with 1tbsp water

Instructions
1. Turn pot on, set to sauté mode. Heat oil in pot, add onions and cook until caramelized.
2. Add water, scraping up any bits.
3. Place roast into pot. Sprinkle ranch dressing and Au Jus gravy mix over meat.
4. Cover pot, lock. Cook on high pressure for 15 minutes.
5. Natural or slow release.
6. Remove meat from pot. Set to sauté mode. Stir in corn starch mixture. Let gravy come to a boil to thicken.
7. Return meat to pot, set to keep warm.

Southwest Chicken Soup

Ingredients
1lb boneless chicken breasts
1tsp salt
½ tsp pepper
1tsp chili powder
1tsp onion powder
1 14.5oz can of fire roasted diced tomatoes or 2 cans of Rote
1 14.5oz can of corn, drained
1 14.5oz can of black beans, rinsed

Instructions
1. Set Instant Pot to sauté mode. Add oil to pot.
2. While waiting for oil to heat, sprinkle dry seasoning mixture over chicken breasts.
3. Once oil is heated, brown both sides of each piece of chicken. Set browned chicken aside.
4. Add tomatoes, to pot, scraping up any brown bits from the bottom. Then add corn, beans and water to pot. Stir and let simmer.
5. Meanwhile, cut chicken breasts into bite-sized cubes. Return chicken to pot. Add more water if desired.
6. Cancel sauté mode. Cover pot with lid. Set to high pressure for 8 minutes. Natural release.
7. Serve hot

Garlic Herbed Chicken

Ingredients

1 lb. boneless chicken breasts or chicken thighs if preferred
½ tsp pepper
½ tsp onion powder
½ tsp thyme
½ tsp basil
½ tsp paprika
1 tsp garlic powder
1 tsp salt
¾ cup water

Instructions

1. Mix dry ingredients together. Rub over chicken.
2. Place steamer rack inside pot. Place chicken on top of rack.
3. Cover, cook on poultry setting or high pressure for 10 minutes. Quick release.

Tip: Save broth at the bottom for other recipes or soup starters. Just be aware this broth might be a more flavorful than canned chicken broth so you might want to cut the salt if using it in other recipes.

Leftover Vegetable Soup

This recipe is perfect for leftover roast, Philly Cheese Steak and Swiss steak

Ingredients
Leftover roast, Philly cheese steak, Swiss steak or any beef entrees
1 bag of baby carrots or 2 large carrots cut into chunks
¼ lb. cut green beans or 1 can green beans
1 medium onion quartered
2 large potatoes cut into large chunks
1 large stalk of celery sliced
2 cups water

Instructions
1. Place leftover and all ingredients in pot. Set to stew.
2. Natural release

Philly Cheese Steak Sandwiches

Ingredients

2 lbs. thin sliced beef cut into strips
1 large green bell pepper sliced
1 large onion sliced
¼ tsp pepper
½ tsp salt
1 tbsp. oil
½ cup water
12 rolls

Instructions

1. Heat oil on sauté mode. Stir in onions and peppers. Cook until onions are caramelized.
2. Remove onions and peppers, set aside.
3. Add beef strips to pot, along with salt and pepper. Stir and let brown slightly. Do not fully cook beef.
4. Add water, and cover pot. Set to cook on high pressure for 5 minutes.
5. Quick release, set pot to sauté to cook down liquid. Once liquid is cooked down, add pepper and onions back into pot. Stir.
6. Serve on rolls.

Chicken Alfredo with Pasta

Ingredients
1 lb. boneless chicken breast halved
1 pack dry Italian seasoning
¾ cup water
1 ½ cup macaroni
Water
1 tbsp. olive oil
½ jar alfredo sauce
1 stainless steel inner pot (for cooking pasta)

Instructions
1. Put ¾ cup water into pot with steamer rack. Set to sauté to bring the water to a boil.
2. While waiting for water to boil, sprinkle italian seasoning over both sides of chicken breast.
3. Place chicken on rack. It's ok to stack the chicken pieces on top of each other.
4. Cancel sauté mode.
5. In the inner pot, place macaroni. Add olive oil and just enough water to cover pasta and about ¼ inch over top. Stir.
6. Place inner pot on top of chicken. Set pot to cook on high pressure for 8 minutes.
7. Quick release.
8. Remove inner pot. Add alfredo sauce to macaroni. Mix well.
9. Remove rack with chicken. Cut into bite-sized chunks.

10. Optional: In a baking dish, add chicken to macaroni, mix well and pop into oven to brown top.

Swiss Steak

Ingredients
2 lbs. cube steak
1 can fire roasted or diced tomatoes
1 medium onion cubed
½ tsp salt
½ tsp paprika
½ tsp garlic powder
1 tsp pepper
1 tbsp. oil

Instructions
1. Mix dry ingredients together. Sprinkle over both sides of steak
2. Turn pot on to sauté mode. Heat oil.
3. Once pot shows as hot, brown steak on both sides still in sauté mode.
4. Remove steak, set aside.
5. Add onions to oil. Cook until softened.
6. Add tomatoes, scraping up browned bits if any. Continue in sauté mode to cook down liquid until tomato mixture is thick.
7. Return steaks to pot, covering meat with thickened tomato mixture.
8. Cover and cook on high pressure for 12 minutes

Jambalaya

Ingredients
1 case sausage
½ lb. raw large shrimp
1 lb. chicken cut into bite sized chunks
1 medium onion finely diced
3 medium bell peppers, finely diced
1 tbsp. creole seasoning
½ tsp salt
1 can crushed tomatoes
2 ½ cups chicken broth
1 ½ cup rice
1 tbsp. oil

Instructions
1. Set pot to sauté mode to heat oil.
2. Add chicken, creole seasoning and salt to heated oil. Brown chicken, remove and set aside.
3. Place onions and bell peppers in pot. Cook until translucent.
4. Return chicken to pot. Add rice, crushed tomatoes and chicken broth. Mix well.
5. Cover and set pot to rice (high pressure at 12 minutes)
6. Quick release. Add sausage in a layer on top of rice. Then place shrimp in a layer on top of sausage.
7. Set pot to cook on manual mode for 2 minutes.
8. Once cooking is done, natural or quick release. Fluff rice, mixing sausage and shrimp well with rice.

www.ingramcontent.com/pod-product-compliance
Lightning Source LLC
Chambersburg PA
CBHW071445070526
44578CB00001B/212